COMPARING TEXTS:
CHALLENGES, APPROACHES AND CONTEXTS

Carol Leach

Nelson Thornes

Published in 2013 by:
Nelson Thornes Ltd
Delta Place
27 Bath Road
CHELTENHAM
GL53 7TH
United Kingdom

13 14 15 16 17 / 10 9 8 7 6 5 4 3 2 1

A catalogue record for this book is available from the British Library

ISBN 978 1 4085 1849 6

Page make-up by OKS Prepress, India

Printed and bound in Spain by GraphyCems

Acknowledgements
With many thanks to Jane Ogborn, for her invaluable support as critic, colleague and friend.

Contents

1 Introduction

Chapter aims

In this chapter we will look at:

- the aims of the book
- what you compare
- why you compare
- understanding Assessment Objectives (AOs).

Key terms

Comparative cross-reference of texts to see the ways in which they are similar and different.

Analysis a structured examination of aspects of your text supported by evidence and your own commentary.

Connections links or common ground between different texts or aspects of text.

Genre a specific type of text. In literature there are three: drama, poetry and prose.

Period a particular time or era in history.

Tone the attitude of the writer to the text itself: for example, formal, playful, sarcastic.

Message(s) opinions, ideas and conclusions that the writer communicates through the text.

Aims of the book

To the student

This book is designed to develop your comparison skills and apply them to the texts you are studying. It examines the ways in which you can approach comparative analysis and provides the help you need to achieve maximum success, whichever examination board you are following. **Read** the book, **use** the guidance and information, **undertake** the activities and **apply** your increased knowledge and understanding to the texts you are studying, and you will better understand how to connect, compare and contrast your texts.

The book provides a key resource to use however it best suits you – for class work, group activities, revision and, significantly, your independent research and development. Its purpose is to focus you on your A Level goals and enhance the comparative study of any of your texts.

One key to academic success at this level is the same as it has always been: an enquiring mind. You have to care. Not only about your A Level result but also about what you do to get it. You have to make meaningful comparisons and connections between your texts.

To the teacher

Using this support material as part of your planning and delivery will provide you with comparative approaches and analyses and their textual applications that are accessible, time-saving, compact and relevant to your Scheme of Work and the teaching of the texts. You will have a key secondary source with pointers for further resources to support your teaching of these texts for comparison.

What you compare

The significant aspects of a literary text are the features that you can identify as the 'building blocks' of any text, whatever their genre or period. You can analyse and compare:

- parts within the whole
- plot and structure
- theme
- setting
- characters and speakers
- form
- language.

Parts within the whole

The first literary comparisons you are likely to consider are the similarities and differences you find within the same text. For example, you can compare:

- how two characters are presented with differing qualities from each other and how these contrasts might show you a way in which the plot or themes develop
- how the use of a particular language technique alters the tone – that contrast might signal a permanent or temporary change in the mood or messages of the text

- how a poet develops similar and different ideas and speakers across different poems within the same collection. Examining that range increases your grasp of the messages of the collection as a whole.

You use the same skills when comparing similarities and differences within one text as you do when comparing two or more texts. You are finding differences and similarities to see what the connections show you about several aspects of the texts you are studying.

Plot and structure

You might think that there is not much to analyse in a plot, as 'who did what when' is not the foundation for comparative analysis of literary texts at A Level. However, an analysis of connections between the plots in your texts can be important.

The plot is more than the story:

1. Plot gives a novel or short story its narrative structure and gives a play its dramatic structure. A story is descriptive and only tells you what happens and to whom. A plot is **dynamic** and organises the story into a structured sequence of events and actions. Identifying a plot can help you to uncover the structures in your texts, particularly in novels, short stories and plays. In poetry, the structure might not be used to tell a story or to deliver a plot, but to present the development or stages of thoughts, feelings and ideas.

2. The execution of the plot and how the story is told can contribute to the presentation of themes – the universal ideas, emotions or messages within and across the texts.

3. Plot can focus on the actions, fortunes and development of characters and their relationships in one or more settings. A comparative analysis of a text's plot could lead to a more detailed grasp of connections between the characters and settings.

4. There can also be more than one plot within the same text and you can compare how the writer uses them: for example, the parallel plots in *Wuthering Heights*, where the story of Cathy and Heathcliff is told alongside the story of young Cathy and Hareton. Each story tells you something about the characters from the other generation and connects the themes of the text overall.

Theme

Within a plot, the writer frames ideas and concepts. These develop as themes alongside the more concrete events of the story and the fortunes and actions of the characters. Where there is no plot, the themes or ideas may express the thoughts and feelings of a speaker. This is typical in poetry, in which a defined plot is often not a necessary part of the poem.

Universal themes

Universal themes deal with the big questions in life that can transcend time or place. You will find that some texts deal with concerns that matter to you now, even if the text was written hundreds of years ago. Because themes can address issues of our shared humanity, you will often find that they support a comparison of texts from different periods and genres. It is

---

Remember

Structure

Structure is a technique – narrative, dramatic or poetic – and it could provide an important comparison of ways in which writers create whole texts.

Did you know?

Poetry, plot and structure
Poetry can have a plot and narrative structure. For example, narrative poems:

- Geoffrey Chaucer, *The Wife of Bath's Prologue and Tale* (*c.*1386–1400)
- John Milton, *Paradise Lost* (1667).

Poetry can use forms from other genres, such as drama. For example, a dramatic monologue presents a sole character who speaks directly to the reader in similar ways that characters in a drama speak to the audience and tell you of their fortunes and actions:

- Carol Ann Duffy, *The World's Wife* (1999)
- Robert Browning, 'My Last Duchess' (1842).

Key terms

Dynamic something which changes, develops or moves.

Narrative poem has two aspects worth remembering:

1. It is designed as a story with a plot and characters.
2. It was the main narrative form before the novel was born.

Dramatic monologue has two aspects worth remembering:
1. It is a piece in which a single speaker addresses an imaginary audience.
2. It has links with lyric poems.

also true that universal themes can mean various things at different times for different societies. For example, love is a universal theme which writers have considered through the ages. The concept of romantic love has never really changed. We can recognise a love story whenever it was written and explore and compare the ways in which the theme of love is presented in the texts. The expression of romantic love, however, can differ from one time or society to another. This could lead to a contrast in how attitudes to love are presented in texts from different times.

Setting

To compare settings, ask yourself the following questions about your texts:

- Are the settings geographical and/or symbolic? Does it matter where it is or what it represents?

- What is the significance of the physical spaces or environments, the weather and climate? How do they develop the mood of the texts?

- Are the settings outdoors or indoors? Are they controlled by society or nature?

- Are there any significant shifts between settings in your texts? Where, when and why do they take place? How do these shifts contribute to the structure and plot in your texts?

- Are there dual settings – for example, two main locations with equal importance in the text? What is the thematic significance of any dual settings?

- How do the settings and any shifts develop the plot, themes and characterisation in the texts?

- How does genre affect the use of setting in your texts?

The interesting thing about settings is that they are so varied in both their presentation and their use. Some writers present setting as a significant feature of the text and use it to perform many of the roles identified in the questions above. Other writers might make little use of setting and concentrate on other aspects of the text to communicate their messages. The comparison of settings is a bit different from aspects such as theme, which is always a central part of the text.

Characters and speakers

It is difficult to analyse your characters and speakers when you approach them as if they are real people. There is only one reason that a character or speaker does or says anything – because that is what the writer wants from their role in the text. Everything that a character or speaker says, does and feels is relevant to their presentation. For example, in drama, their presence or absence on stage is deliberate. In a novel, a row in a relationship is significant. In a poem, the feelings expressed through a speaker, or voice, are important to the way in which the poet creates the mood of the poem. The speech, actions and relationships of a character or speaker are constructed deliberately. They show you the ideas and themes that the writer develops as the plot or text progresses. Comparing the behaviour and motivations of characters or speakers will support your analysis of themes and messages across the texts.

Form

When you compare form, you are analysing ways that the texts are shaped externally, as a whole. For example, the sonnet, the tragedy and the science-fiction novel are all examples of literary subgenres, each of which has its own form. This is different from an analysis of structure. Structure shapes the texts internally and shows how a form or subgenre is put together, part by part. Your comparison of form helps with your overview of each text as a whole.

Form is linked to context, as each form has its roots and popularity in a particular place and time. This means that form can sometimes reflect typical styles from the era in which the text was written or performed – for example, Jacobean revenge tragedy, Romantic poetry, Victorian realist novels, Trench poetry. Sometimes the formal roots or eras of your texts are more hazy or diverse. If context is less significant in your comparison, it is more important to focus on how form shapes the ideas in the texts and your responses to them. Sometimes so many forms influence texts from the late 20th century, especially novels and drama, that we refer to their blended use as hybrid forms. For example, post-1990 plays such as Tony Kushner's *Angels in America* (1992) or Diane Samuels' *Kindertransport* (1995), and novels such as *Behind the Scenes at the Museum* (1995) by Kate Atkinson or *The Ghost Road* (1995) by Pat Barker, all use a range of forms at the same time.

Language

The importance of comparing language is to see how a writer uses words and punctuation:

- to deliver the plot and/or themes and ideas
- to construct characters or speakers
- to set the mood and tone
- to use or adapt conventions of form, structure and subgenre.

The analysis of language is sometimes presented as a difficult task or skill because it requires detailed knowledge about how language works and what role it has in the text you are studying. However, time spent on language analysis will help you to see what the writer is creating overall. For example, your analysis of a character or speaker will make sense if you look at how language is used to present them.

You can also look at how language connects texts that are written:

- at the same time to show how they are products of their era (and genre or form)
- in different genres and times, which might show how they have similar concerns and themes, even if they have different styles of language use.

For example, you can compare how Carol Ann Duffy and Sheenagh Pugh use some similar techniques that are typical of post-1990 poetry. You can explore ways in which *The Color Purple* (1982) by Alice Walker and *Wuthering Heights* (1847) by Emily Brontë use accent, dialect and colloquial language. You could compare how their characters in each setting show us something about social attitudes in their eras. You might want to analyse the ways in which *Wuthering Heights* has connections with a 17th-century play, such as John Webster's *The White Devil* (1609–12) and a late 20th-century short

Key terms

Subgenre a division within a genre, such as science fiction or tragedy.

Context a range of factors affecting how texts are written, received and understood.

Hybrid a product whose style has blended two or more styles into a new product.

Accent the way words are pronounced according to geographical setting or social class.

Dialect the language variety of a geographical setting or social class.

Colloquial language informal, casual, conversational words and phrases; language that you might speak yourself.

story, such as Angela Carter's 'The Bloody Chamber' (1979). You could compare how they explore ideas about revenge and cruelty through violent and bloodthirsty language.

Why you compare

There are two main reasons to compare literary texts at A Level:

1. You will develop the skill of seeing how texts fit together in a tradition or fall outside of a typical pattern, and how they learn from and influence each other. When you grasp what a particular writer is trying to do at a given point in the text, you can develop your understanding of that text by looking at what other writers are also trying to do. This comparison or contrast works whether the texts are from the same or different times, or in the same or different genres and subgenres.

2. You will meet the requirements of your course of study.

You can achieve both of these goals if you understand the Assessment Objectives and how comparing texts is part of them.

Understanding Assessment Objectives (AOs)

At A Level English Literature, the Assessment Objectives are:

- AO1: Articulate creative, informed and relevant responses to literary texts, using appropriate terminology and concepts, and coherent, accurate written expression

- AO2: Demonstrate detailed critical understanding in analysing the ways in which structure, form and language shape meanings in literary texts

- AO3: Explore connections and comparisons between different literary texts, informed by interpretations of other readers

- AO4: Demonstrate understanding of the significance and influence of the contexts in which literary texts are written and received.

The primary focus for this book is the first part of AO3 and its application to the study and assessment of your texts: 'Explore connections and comparisons between different literary texts'.

It will also help you to get to grips with the other AOs and to see how comparative analysis can be linked to a shared context (AO4), a shared use of subject matter (AO1) and a shared use of technique (AO2).

How AOs work

The AOs are a guide to ensure that:

- you have consistent opportunities to develop the appropriate skills for A Level study in each lesson and study experience

- you have consistent opportunities to demonstrate the appropriate skills for A Level study in each essay you write

- the set examination questions always focus on the topic and skill areas that your course has outlined

- the coursework tasks designed by you and your teachers always focus on the topic and skill areas that your course has outlined.

Applying AOs to essay writing

AOs set out the ways in which you will be assessed in your examinations. They also help you to check that you are on the right track in your course of study. If you are being assessed in a particular AO, you must demonstrate how you have developed that skill throughout your course of assessment as instructed in your examination board's specification.

So if you know that AO3 is worth half the marks in the essay you must write for a particular exam text or section or coursework task, your written demonstration of the importance of comparisons and connections between your texts is vital. You will need to:

- show that any comparisons you make with other texts are valid and support the relevant ideas in the question and your argument (AO3)
- embed the comparisons and contrasts in your texts throughout your answer in a clearly structured and substantial way. Even if the AO3 is only worth 10 per cent of the answer, you still need to do this, but perhaps less substantially, so that you also focus on what else is being assessed (AO3)
- trace the key words of the question from your introduction until your conclusion, linking the specifically identified comparative issue(s) to the relevant evidence in your text (AO1)
- prove how each comparison shows the reader something specific about the particular part of the text you are using (AO1)
- show how your opinion, or your debate of the opinion of others, is relevant to the ideas in the question (AO3)
- select the relevant contextual information that is demonstrated in your text (AO4)
- organise your argument to show all this to your reader. Avoid distracting or irrelevant contexts, text references, opinions and comparisons that take the focus away from what you want to say, in response to this particular task or question (all AOs, especially the skills of relevance and coherence, AO1).

Applying AOs to examination questions

A Level examination questions are always very specific in their wording and in what they require from you. It is important that you take the time to identify the key words and how they signal which AOs are being assessed, and then plan and structure an answer that responds **only** to the key words. Here are some examples of questions from A Level English Literature papers in 2012:

AQA A (AS)

[Texts: contextual linking of an unseen non-fiction extract to your studied texts. For example, wider reading of a range of twentieth- and twenty-first-century texts from any genre]
How does the writer present his thoughts and feelings about the struggle for identity?
How far is the extract similar to and different from your wider reading about the struggle for identity in modern literature? You should consider the writer's choices of form, structure and language, as well as subject matter.

OCR (A2)

[Focus: one drama and one poetry text, pre-1800. For example, *Songs of Innocence and of Experience* (1794) by William Blake and *The White Devil* (1609–12) by John Webster]
'Laughter is always dangerous.'
In the light of this view, discuss ways in which writers use humour. In your answer, compare one drama text and one poetry text from the above lists.

> **Key term**
>
> **Unseen** a text or extract used in some examination questions, but not set for classroom study or preparation.

Critical discussion analysis that weighs up the ideas in the question, according to different interpretations (yours and/or other readers or critics) of the text.

Subject matter what the text is about: its plot, themes and ideas.

WJEC (AS)

[Focus: two poetry texts. For example, *Selected Poems* (1994) by Carol Ann Duffy and *Selected Poems* (1990) by Sheenagh Pugh]
What connections have you found between the ways in which Duffy and Pugh write about desire in their poems? In your response you must include detailed **critical discussion** of at least **two** of Duffy's poems.

AQA B (A2)

[Focus: three texts from any genre, including one from before 1800. For example, 'Elements of the Gothic' including *The White Devil* (1609–12) by John Webster, *Wuthering Heights* (1847) by Emily Brontë and *The Bloody Chamber* (1979) by Angela Carter]
To what extent do you agree with the view that, in gothic writing, death is the punishment for sin?

Edexcel (AS)

[Focus: *Wuthering Heights* (1847) and either *The Scarlet Letter* (1850) or *The Color Purple* (1982)]
'The main problem with this tale is that it gives us no-one to like.'
Explore the methods writers use to present characters whom we may like or dislike.
In your response, you should focus on *Wuthering Heights* to establish your argument and you should refer to the second text you have read to support and develop your line of argument.

Activity 1

Linking AOs to questions and this book

1. Consider the examination questions above. Remind yourself of the title and aims of this book.

2. Identify the key words in the exam questions. Identify to which AO each one belongs – for example, **subject matter**/AO1, technique/AO2, context/AO4.

3. Look again at the key words in the questions that you identified as references to AO3/comparisons and connections. Make a list of the comparisons and connections being examined. What aspects of the texts are being compared and connected?

Activity 1 shows how the relationship between AOs and questions works to help you to maximise your exam success. When you understand what is being assessed and how it is asked, you are halfway to applying the relevant skills appropriately in the allocated time.

Examiner's tip

'Stretch and challenge'
Candidates who demonstrate how their studies 'stretch and challenge' them at A Level English Literature use the following high-order skills in their examination essays:

- making meaningful comparisons, connections and cross-references that range across and within the relevant texts (AO3)

- making relevant use of shared contexts across the texts (AO4)

- moving confidently between general and specific details (all AOs).

Summary

This chapter has introduced the ways in which this book can help you develop your comparison skills and apply them to the texts you are studying. You should now have more understanding of:

- what you compare

- why you compare

- Assessment Objectives (AOs).

2 How context affects comparisons

The importance of context

It is likely that the texts you compare will have some shared contexts. Your knowledge of their shared contexts enhances the connections you can make between your texts. Even when you compare a feature that appears to be internal to your texts, such as language, the external connections you find may provide further links to support detailed comparisons and help you to develop a comparative overview of your texts.

Making context relevant to comparison

Texts can tell us about the world and society in which they were written, and sometimes about the one we live in now – even if they were written in a different time and/or place. You also need to consider how your own contexts affect your contemporary understanding and interpretation of your texts.

Let us think about something that affects us now in British society: think of your favourite music. Maybe you thought of a song that you like. Now think about what you know about the singer or band. How did you find this out? If they are releasing music currently, you have probably heard or seen them in the mass media. You might know about:

- their style – how they look, dress, talk and pose – which could influence whether or how much they appeal to you
- where they come from, how they live and what they stand for. Maybe you feel somehow connected with them or that you share something in common. Maybe you feel that they 'speak to you' by representing your generation or social group, and generating ideas that you are, or would like to be, part of. Maybe you feel they have captured a moment for you or are reacting against one that you too react against.

If any of this is true, you might have chosen to find out more about the singer or band beyond what is obvious from a first look or listen. If you have, you are attaching importance to something about them that goes beyond the song, in order to enhance your pleasure or knowledge of what you already like and know. You are linking the song to the circumstances in which it has been created and produced. You are seeking to put the song into context.

How we receive and compare

You might also want to contextualise the song because the singer or band is important or appealing to your contemporaries (your own friends and peers) and you want to be knowledgeable about this specific aspect of the culture that surrounds you – you want to engage with the reception of the song. This might lead you to explore (**to cross-reference and compare**), through experience and research, other similar bands and singers, to see what they are part of and if you would like their contemporaries as well. You might also be interested in how your favourite band or singer sounds like an earlier band or singer who seem to have influenced them, or even another contemporary band or singer whom they have influenced themselves.

How context supports comparison

The contexts that you have explored might be about the **lives and behaviours** of the singer or band, their musical **genre and style**, their **musical and historical era**, their ideology, their **fame and popularity** at a particular time, or the influences and connections they demonstrate.

Key terms

Typicality where several texts share common or similar contexts, especially within the same period.

Contemporary something happening within its own time. This can be in the past or the present. For example, First World War contemporary matters are those happening in that period. Today's contemporary issues are those happening now, at this moment.

Reception how we experience, understand and receive ideas, products and events.

Ideology political, social and cultural beliefs and ideas.

Why it matters

Applying this process to any type of artistic product from any period in time may seem daunting, remote or even meaningless. But if you find out more about the factors that created the products, you are more likely to understand, and perhaps better enjoy and appreciate, the product itself and some others that are like it – or even different from it. This works just as well with products that you dislike. Sometimes it justifies your dislike, sometimes it affects your initial opinion or reaction and your reception of the product is modified as a result of your increased contextual knowledge and understanding.

Comparing contexts at A Level

You are studying an A Level that incorporates the otherwise everyday activity of exploring the significance of context in your own life and times, as described above in the music example. A Level study involves an appreciation of factors that have contextual significance, in just the same way as with music: literary texts are not created in isolation, any more than your favourite music came to fruition in outer space. Literature is of its own time and world and is inseparable from it, and, like music, is socially and culturally inter-connected with its contemporaries. Your response to the music and the musicians, or the texts and the writers, has as much to do with your time and world as it does with theirs.

Your texts can also be connected to texts from different periods, because literary contexts remain relevant through many periods of time.

To enhance your comparative analysis of texts, we can explore the following contexts as shown in the table.

Types of context	Focus
historical, social, political, cultural	time, world/society and beliefs
literary	styles and genres
biographical	lives and circumstances
reception	your reactions to these factors

The context of reception

Reception and time

From what point in time do you consider a text to be either 'old' or 'contemporary'? Before you were born? Centuries ago? In the last few years? The reception of a text, its relevance and its accessibility can change, even after just one generation of readers and audiences. On the other hand, it is sometimes easier to receive the core messages of a text if you are looking back on its issues or styles, even if it is only ten years later.

Sometimes, however, obscure cultural references and difficult language affect your initial reception of a text from another period. As you study the text, familiarity changes your understanding of what the writer has to say to you. When you compare texts from different eras, the context of reception is a significant factor in your analysis.

Remember

Context and you

How you experience a text has as much to do with your own context as the context of the text itself. Reception of text is part of your personal response: your critical opinion of the texts (AO3).

Activity 1

Reception and you

Make a list of the last three texts you have read or seen performed. They do not have to be the ones you are studying. You can include film and TV adaptations.

1. Identify the subject matter. Compare your response to its presentation in each text or performance. How and why were your reactions similar and/or different?

2. Identify the characters that you found significant or interesting, or to which you had a strong reaction. Compare your responses to each of them. Where do your sympathies lie? How and why were your reactions similar and/or different?

3. Compare your responses to the setting or moods of the texts. How and why were your reactions similar and/or different?

Typicality

To examine what your texts have in common and how they compare, you can investigate their shared contexts by looking for features that are typical. For example, if they are from different eras, there may be some typicality of style for you to compare.

One way to compare how context influences your texts is to explore how the texts are impacted by the world outside, and then work your way in to the particular details through the styles of your text and writer. You could examine typicality of period or style by comparing the following contextual factors:

- **historical and political** contexts influence every event and person in the period or 'times'
- **social and cultural** contexts influence some events and groups of people in the society
- **biographical** contexts concern the life and circumstances of an individual
- **literary** contexts express the styles and concerns of the period, society or individual writer.

By comparing and contrasting these different contextual elements, you will be able to identify ways in which typical elements of the texts make them part of a specific tradition. You will also be able to see if they stand outside the norm and are viewed as different from the typical texts of their period, genre or style.

Historical and political contexts
Developing an overview

A grasp of the historical and political contexts gives you some overview of the world outside the texts. This will help you to understand the issues and ideas within the texts themselves. You might want to compare what was, and could still be, happening during the period, and how it might be important to your comparison of the texts you are studying. Applying to a literary text the importance of a period or movement in time is a key part of how A Level Literature courses are designed.

Understanding the historical and political contexts helps you to tackle AO3 (interpretation and comparisons) with more confidence. With some knowledge of the period, you can:

- develop and cross-refer your own ideas and beliefs
- weigh up other ideas
- see which ideas you accept or reject as ways into the texts
- weigh up how you receive the contexts themselves.

Social contexts

Social context usually refers to what we believe people are doing and thinking in any given era, and how society functions and organises itself, and develops social trends and fashions to mirror its ideologies. Society (people in groups and as individuals) both creates and responds to the large-scale events and movements of the history that we receive and learn. Society creates, rejects or challenges contemporary political systems. Social contexts can form important comparisons of the ways that the values, customs and behaviours of a particular time and place are presented in the text.

Cultural contexts

Cultural contexts create a bridge between the historical, political and social contexts and the literary and biographical contexts. How does this bridge work, and what do we mean by 'culture'?

Culture and literature

Culture embraces literary contexts as it includes art movements and all art forms. For example, the Modernists are a group of North American and European writers, including the American poet T.S. Eliot, the English novelist Virginia Woolf and the German playwright Bertolt Brecht. Modernist writers all share some cultural ideas that influenced the development of their particular creative styles during the early 20th century. Their ideology and their subject matter were reflected in the literature, paintings, design and music of the time. This example of Modernism – a cultural movement that includes literary contexts – demonstrates how the relationship between culture and literature can operate, and how ideas about typicality can help you to compare aspects of your texts.

Biographical contexts

Making connections

Before you compare the significance of biographical contexts in your texts, consider whether any of the following factors are important:

- **Where are your writers from?** Even if they are contemporaries and have some shared contexts, they often have disparate cultural and geographical backgrounds and origins.

- **How old are your writers?** The writers of the texts you study might have been born at significantly different times in terms of their era's history, politics, society and culture. For example, a 'post-1990 writer' might have been either 20 or 70 when they wrote your post-1990 text. This aspect of his or her biography will affect how other contexts influence the text.

- **Which styles do they use?** The writers you study might have literary connections with each other, whatever period they come from, and you can explore these as a vital part of your comparisons between writers and texts. They are also separate individuals who use many different styles.

- **Who and what influences their choices of style and genre?** Is there anything in the first two bullet points that could affect their choices?

Confusing life with literature

Biographical contexts can be a hindrance as well as a help. Familiarity with a writer's biography can make it harder to get a historical (or even a social) perspective on their work, their legacies and their influences. You can become distracted by their personalities, instead of focusing on what makes their work important within their era or style. Even if the text is autobiographical, knowledge of your writers' lives can limit your literary response to the text. You might become tempted to describe the writers' life story, guess 'their' feelings and try to fit biographical meaning to aspects of the text, when literary contexts and language techniques might provide a better starting point.

Similarly, using social identity as a biographical context can reduce the complexity or individuality of your writer's achievements. Do you categorise or compare your writers according to social labels? This can be useful for considering the historical or cultural contexts but many writers reject being identified by categories based on biological social or even geographical factors.

Literary contexts

Approaches to literary contexts

You can examine how literary contexts (AO4) can be compared in your texts by using the following questions as a guide. The examples given are just for reference and will be covered in more detail later in the book.

1. What do your writers write about? For example: the First and Second World Wars, across all genres and from the period of the war until the present day.
   (Subject matter – AO1)

2. How do your writers use techniques of language, form and structure to express the literary and cultural ideas of the time? For example: split-narrative forms, especially in novels and plays; free verse in poetry.
   (Style – AO2)

3. How are genre and subgenre used? For example: in novels, the bildungsroman; in poetry, the sonnet; in drama, tragedy.
   (Style – AO2)

4. Which cultural and artistic movements have influenced and shaped your texts? For example: Modernism, across the genres; Romanticism, especially in poetry; Absurdism, especially in drama.
   (Cultural contexts – AO4)

5. Which literary traditions have influenced and shaped your texts? For example: which writers are included in the Western literary canon (the 'list' of accepted, respected and studied texts), or how intertextuality is used.
   (Literary history/historical contexts – AO4)

6. How can the mood, tone and viewpoints appear to be 'typical' of your texts as a part of their era or style? For example: the self-aware or self-questioning styles of end-of-millennium novels, such as Ian McEwan's *Enduring Love,* or the ghosts and madness you find in a Jacobean revenge tragedy.
   (Literary styles and political and social contexts – AO2 and AO4)

Literary heritage

Literary contexts influence writers in the production of their texts because the novelist, dramatist or poet is part of a long line of literature that has gone before, a heritage of thousands of years.

A text can have more than one literary context because it can be influenced by a range of techniques and subgenres across time. This increases the connections you can make between your texts as it multiplies the possible connections. It also multiplies the differences, so always avoid generalisations about a typical style and its use in the text.

> ### Remember
>
> **Comparing literary contexts**
> Literary contexts are the factors that apply to literary texts and identify them as such. Literary contexts only apply to literature – unlike, for example, political contexts, which influence all walks of life in the given era, from literature to sport to town planning to health policy. Consequently, examining literary contexts always takes you to the detail that your comparative analysis will need.

> ### Key terms
>
> **Western literary canon** a body of literature throughout history and across genres that the Western academic establishment considers as classics for all time and core texts for study.
>
> **Intertextuality**
> 1. When a text responds to ideas, language or direct references adopted or adapted from an earlier text.
> 2. Where a writer refers to another person's work or textual innovations within his or her own text.

> ### Activity 2
>
> **Revisiting examination questions**
> In Chapter 1, Activity 1, you linked AOs to the key words of some exam questions, and the title and aims of this book.
>
> Look again at those examination questions (pages 9–10). Identify where context is part of the comparison targeted in each question.

> ### Summary
>
> This chapter has introduced the types of context that can help you to compare any texts you study. You should now have more understanding of:
>
> - the importance of context
> - typicality in your texts.

3 How to compare

Comparing periods

As you know, period is the time or era in which a text is written or a drama is first performed. To make comparisons between your texts, you can examine the ways in which they reflect or challenge the period they are from and see if this provides you with connections to analyse.

Finding similarities

You might find that texts from the same period have similar concerns or subject matter, influenced by their historical and political, social and cultural contexts as part of the typicality of their time. This can form the starting point for your comparison. Texts from the same period might use genre and subgenre in similar ways as part of the literary contexts that influence the time of writing. If your texts are from a different period, they could still have some similarities in their concerns and subject matter if the writers address universal themes and ideas that remain important across time.

Finding differences

You might find that texts from different periods present their view of the world in very different ways, as they are directly influenced by contemporary ideologies and the thoughts and behaviours of the society in which they live. Differences in period can lead to differences in the ways that writers deliver their messages and ideas or respond to their literary and cultural contexts. Even within the same period, texts do not have one uniform context. The writers may share the same history, but might come from different social backgrounds or identify with different cultures within the period. This element of difference can be reflected in the influence of a cultural movement on the production of the texts. Even within the same period and cultural movement, they might choose to adopt and develop different styles.

Comparing genres

Finding similarities

You will find that texts from the same genre – novels and short stories, drama or poetry – broadly follow a set of recognisable conventions that are typical of their genre. For example, drama is designed to be performed. What you study is the script that actors and directors use to create the physical, live experience of the play that you watch as an audience. The novel or short story, like a play, often involves characters in a plot, but also draws on the reader's imagination to create a visual picture. It has more opportunity to describe and develop the world inhabited by the characters, often through extensive narrative details of their personalities and the settings around them. Poetry is designed to communicate situations and events, thoughts and feelings, where every word is used to convey the maximum meaning possible. Often strict and tight forms can determine how many lines or words can be used. The similarities evident in these literary conventions act as a good starting point for your comparison, as they show how each genre typically presents feelings, ideas and stories.

You might find that different genres have the same subject matter and concerns – plot, themes and ideas. They may have similar settings, moods and tone. These similarities can be especially significant if the texts are from the same period, have shared contexts and demonstrate a typicality of their era and styles. The same similarities can also apply to texts that have been written centuries apart, even if their contexts are different.

Sometimes, the different structures of contrasting genres can be used for similar purposes in your texts. For example, both structures could use the first part to introduce you to a character who dies at the midpoint and is succeeded by their enemy or mourned by a loved one. Despite the different genres, you might be encouraged to feel sympathy for the character who dies in both cases. You might find, for example, that even though one text is a novel and the other a drama, both use the conventions of tragedy to present a central character.

Finding differences

If you study texts from different genres you might find that the literary features are used in different ways. You can examine whether the different structures of the genres you study have a different purpose in the texts. For example, the structure of a poem is significant from line to line and verse to verse. Some poetic forms have specific structures with conventional uses, such as a sonnet to debate love or a ballad to tell the story of someone's misfortunes. A play divided into acts and scenes might rely on its dramatic structure to present the passage of time or to shift locations as part of the plot and character development. The passage of time or location could be incidental to a sonnet or a ballad.

Comparing subgenres

If you are studying texts from the same genre and notice that they use the literary features in very different ways, it is likely that they either come from a different period or use different subgenres.

Even within the same genre, there is considerable variety of subgenres. For example, the drama genre has many subgenres, just between the years 1590 and 1640. Revenge tragedy is an important and popular dramatic subgenre of this period. The many subgenres – for example, different types of tragedy, comedy and history – make the drama genre varied in this period. Contemporary drama has even more varied subgenres and characteristically does not conform to traditional subgenres of tragedy, comedy or history. The tragedy subgenre itself had undergone significant changes by the early 20th century. The overall drama genre is **unified** (or similar) through its genre conventions, as part of its literary contexts. It is also **varied** (or different), as a result of its subgenres and the specific conventions of each of these, which can change over time, as part of a more detailed literary context.

Finding similarities

If you compare texts from the same genre and period, you can examine how your texts use the specific features of their subgenre. If you compare texts from the same genre and different periods, you can investigate if similar subgenres have influenced both texts across time.

Link

For more information on which literary features to compare, see Chapter 1, pages 4–8.

Key terms

Tragedy a form of drama concerned with human suffering and multiple deaths, traditionally caused partly by the flaws of the tragic hero(ine).

Sonnet 14 lines of iambic pentameter verse. Different types of sonnet follow particular rhyme schemes.

Ballad a song that tells a story, originally set to music, with basic rhythms to make it easy to remember and to sing.

Revenge tragedy a tragedy play that focuses on the motive, planning and execution of death by revenge, usually involving multiple deaths.

Comedy a form of drama with a happy or satisfying outcome for the plot and its main characters.

History a form of drama that focuses on historical events which often acted as military or royal propaganda or criticism.

Did you know?

Gothic literature

The Gothic subgenre has a set of recognised features drawn from a hybrid of horror and romance subgenres. It remains popular across literary genres (especially in film) and connects texts from very different periods in time.

Think about it

Originality and comparison

In some cases, a work or a writer is believed to be culturally unique. Can you think of anyone whose work you have read who you might apply this to, or any text that you would describe as 'unique'?

Remember

Shall I compare thee?

When two texts are so different that there is nothing similar about their period, genre or use of subgenres, you will struggle to make meaningful comparisons. Not all texts can be usefully connected.

Texts from different genres can also draw on similar or identical subgenres. Some of the literary features might operate differently, such as structure and form, but others, such as themes, setting and language, may have significant connections. For example, the literary subgenre of Gothic literature is a cultural and artistic movement inspired by Gothic styles in literature, painting, architecture and the landscape gardens of country houses. It originates from the 18th-century Romantic and 19th-century Victorian eras and ideologies. The most famous, or typical, Gothic literary texts of the period are novels, such as Jane Austen's *Northanger Abbey* (1817), Mary Shelley's *Frankenstein* (1818) and Emily Brontë's *Wuthering Heights* (1847). The poet Coleridge also uses features of the Gothic style in his long, narrative poem, 'The Rime of the Ancient Mariner' (1798). Even texts from the 16th century have been described as using features of Gothic style, such as the play *Doctor Faustus* (1594) by Christopher Marlowe.

Finding differences

Texts that share period, genre and even subgenre can still demonstrate differences. It is rare to find identical texts, even if they present several similarities and typicalities of their era and style. Unless they only mimic the work of another writer, an individual writer will have his or her own influences and contexts, so some difference is inevitable. When you are comparing texts, what is important is to find the significant differences that impact on the product, the text itself, to create a new work. It might be at this detailed level that you start to uncover some original literary texts that were ground-breaking or innovative when they were written. The comparative element of such work might be related to their influence, or as an outstanding or complex example of a more ordinary literary movement or style.

Activity 1

Setting up how to compare

Consider the texts you want to compare.

1. Identify the period, genre and subgenre of each text.

2. Identify any contexts that might have influenced the period, genre and subgenres.

3. Examine any similarities and differences that you find across your texts at this stage.

4. Identify any significant similarities and differences in the ways in which each text uses literary features: for example, how the main character is presented or where the text is set.

5. Find three examples of how each text uses language in order to support your findings in question 4.

Making connections between texts

How to uncover comparisons

To find similarities or differences in texts from any period and genre, a good starting point is to identify, examine and explore:

- shared subject matter – plot, themes, ideas and messages (AO1): what does each writer write about?

- shared techniques – writers' use of language, form, structure, subgenre, genre (AO2): how do they write? What are the effects of the techniques each writer uses in the texts?

- shared contexts – historical and political, social and cultural, literary (AO4): how do contexts influence each text and the ways it has been written?

- shared responses – your interpretation and the interpretations of other readers (AO3): how and why do you and other people respond to the texts?

- how does your exploration of the shared features above form the basis for a comparison of your texts (AO3): what connections can you make?

How to structure comparisons

If you have used the above bullet points as a starting point for making connections, you will need to structure your notes and ideas into a meaningful response, and eventually an essay, for the exam or coursework task. You have two choices:

1. Write about the subject matter, techniques, contexts and interpretations of one text you are studying, followed by your response to these aspects of the other text/s. This approach can be problematic. However well you plan your answer, it is difficult to use this method and make meaningful comparisons between the texts without repeating what you have written on a previous text or leaping ahead to the next one.

2. Explore the similarities and differences in one aspect of all the texts, such as subject matter. Then move on to the next aspect, such as language or a specific context, making sure that it links with or moves on from the previous aspect that you considered. This way, you will not waste time repeating yourself. The structure of your comparative analysis will be neater and you will appear more confident and in control of your material and expression – which always means more marks for AO1.

Whichever method you choose, the key to a successful comparative analysis is to keep it relevant throughout your response.

> ### Examiner's tip
>
> **Avoid repeating yourself**
> If you use phrases like 'As I mentioned earlier…' it is likely that you are repeating yourself. This will not increase your mark, as there is nothing new to reward in your response.

> ### Summary
>
> This chapter has explored the types of context that can help you to compare any text you study. You should now have more understanding of:
>
> - how to compare periods
> - how to compare genres
> - how to compare subgenres
> - how to make connections between texts.

4 Same genre, same period

Chapter aims

In this chapter we will look at how to compare texts from the same genre and period. We will consider:

- poetry
- prose
- drama.

Identifying similarities and differences

When you compare texts from the same genre, you can analyse any shared technical features of that genre. When those texts are also written at the same time or during the same era, you can see how particular techniques were popular at the time. You can also compare how writers with many shared contexts respond to important subject matter and ideas that are within their society.

Finding similarities

Texts from the same genre and period share many themes and features. You might find several clear connections to uncover and address across the Assessment Objectives in response to your texts. There can be many similarities between texts by writers from the same time and place, who choose the same genre to communicate their ideas and concerns. Look for:

- shared concerns and/or themes (AO1): how writers respond to shared cultural, social and political contexts (AO4)
- shared techniques (AO2): how writers respond to shared cultural and literary contexts (AO4).

Finding differences

You will always find differences between your texts. Writers can respond very differently to the same events in time and can choose very different techniques (even within the same genre and period) to convey their responses.

Sometimes it is their different ideologies that lead to different responses within the same genre and period. Sometimes the literary contexts are diverse. Even if the texts were written in the same town and year, by writers with the same ideology, age, social class, gender, race, sexuality, and so on, each text needs to be approached as an individual work if you want your comparisons to be meaningful. You can explore any significant differences between your same-genre/same-period texts in the same way that you explore their similarities. Examine these differences:

- their concerns and/or themes (AO1): where writers respond as individuals to their cultural, social and political contexts (AO4)
- their use of techniques (AO2): where writers respond as individuals to their cultural and literary contexts (AO4).

Poetry

Finding similarities

Even when your texts share a common genre and period, a good starting point in exploring similarities between your chosen texts is to go to the text itself. Important shared contexts that influence the texts will arise from your analysis of the poetry itself.

If you are studying whole poetry collections you need to get an overview of the range and variety of subjects, themes and styles that each poet chooses. Explore what connects poems from the same collection and consider the

Links

For more information on what you compare and how to apply the Assessment Objectives, see Chapter 1, pages 4–10.

For more information on making connections between your texts, see Chapter 3, pages 16–19.

significance of the ways that they are grouped and ordered. When you have some knowledge and understanding of how each collection fits together as a whole text, you can select individual poems for a comparative analysis. You will need to compare individual poems from each collection, rather than making general comparisons between the two collections. You can start with a general comparison – for example, Sheenagh Pugh and Carol Ann Duffy have both written dramatic monologues. You can use this similarity as a starting point to uncover further similarities the poems may share. Analyse how each writer uses and adapts the form and how the individual poems look and sound to the reader as a result.

Finding differences

The best way to identify difference is to work from the similarities first. Find what your poems have in common. From here, you will uncover aspects of each poem that do not match or share a feature. Use these differences to examine how the poems also contrast, despite their connections. Although Duffy and Pugh both write dramatic monologues and are writing within the same period, they use the dramatic monologue form in different ways. Pugh goes so far to say that she does not know why A Level study compares her poetry with that of Duffy, as she believes they have nothing in common. Many disagree and see similarities in their work and connections between individual poems that make them comparable. Later in this chapter, you can decide for yourself (see Activity 2 on page 28).

The variety of poems within a collection can mean that some poems make better comparisons than others. Some poems from one collection might have nothing to compare with some poems from another collection. It is important that you choose examples that can usefully answer the question or topic that you are tackling. This is especially important for comparative poetry analysis, as you need to pay particular attention to poetic language.

What to compare

Consider this method for finding similarities and differences in poetry from the same genre and the same period.

Subject matter

Explore the subject matter of the poems to examine common elements. Use these questions to compare what the poems are about and any settings for their subject matter.

- What is each poem is about?
- Is there a plot or story, a sequence of events – a narrative element?
- Is there a depiction of a person/people? Do the poems give you details about how they feel, think, look, move, and so on – a descriptive element?
- Does the narrative or descriptive element appear to be about the speaker, or persona, of the poem?
- Are the poems about a place or landscape – a setting? Are the settings imaginary or physical places? If there is a physical place, is it named? Is it somewhere the speaker has visited or lived? If it is an imaginary place, is it a fantasy? Are they about what happens in the mind or human body? Is there a journey?
- What ideas and concerns do the poets present to you?

Examiner's tip

Finding similarities across collections

Do base your comparisons on close readings of what you find in the text itself.

Do not 'find similarities' by trying to fit the poetry to general themes and forms you have found elsewhere in the collection. If you do this, your comparison will be superficial and may even be inaccurate.

Technique

Explore **how** the subject matter of the poems is presented to the reader.

Viewpoint

- Identify the roles of any speakers.
- What relationships are they attempting to create with you? Do they speak to you directly?
- Are you invited to observe a third party and/or given intimate details about the speakers themselves?
- Who created that viewpoint – the speaker/s or the poets? What is the difference between these two viewpoints?

Language

- What types of language are being used? For example, is it formal, colloquial or slang?
- How does the type of language affect the presentation of subject matter?
- What are the effects of the use of individual words, phrases or groups of words with a similar meaning or function? For example, the use of verbs and any adverbs.
- How does the language use affect your responses to the poems?

Exploring how language is used in the texts you are comparing is especially important in this genre. Poetic language is always highly significant, as each word is expected to do so much work. In poetry, there is usually a more condensed use of language, which requires your close attention to how the poet 'shapes meaning'. The comparison of poetry might hinge on how techniques are used in a few lines, such as repetition or the use of colloquialisms.

Form

- Are you comparing how traditional forms are used and/or adapted? Why?
- Are you comparing examples of free verse?
- Is there anything important to compare about how the form and structure illuminate the messages and ideas in each poem?

Structure

- Do they conform to a particular literary form?
- Do the structures have a regular pattern?
- Are the structures used to divide or develop the messages and subject matter into a particular sequence? How? For example, with the use of turning points and breaks in poems. Why?
- How are the line endings significant? What is the effect of ending an idea at the end of a line or continuing it onto the next line or verse?

Sound features

- How important is the sound of the poems?
- Do they depend on rhythm, rhyme, the spoken voice, pace, pauses or moments of silence, for example, in order to communicate the subject matter, messages and mood?

Think about it

Evoking emotion in the reader

The poet Daljit Nagra believes that abstract nouns and adjectives, such as 'beauty' and 'beautiful', should not be used in poetry. Instead, he says that poets should describe what they see. The reader can then decide how each image evokes emotions, contextualised by their own reception of the poem. How does this idea affect your reading of the poetry extracts on pages 24, 26 and 27? What about your own poems?

Key terms

Colloquialisms informal, casual, conversational words and phrases; language that you might use yourself.

Free verse poetry written without the rules of rhyme, stanza pattern or metre, with no predetermined form so any new shape is possible

Tackling technique

Do not be afraid of technique. Technique simply means the tools the poet uses in order to convey their subject matter and/or message. Try not to reduce it to a tedious checklist of technical terms (such as alliteration, enjambment and repetition) to tick off, without knowing why you are comparing them. What matters to your comparative poetry analysis is the effect that each technique used has on the poem. Remember that nothing the poet does is by accident. Whether you compare two or more poems or are selecting from across two or more collections, your comparison must be based on detailed evidence from the texts themselves. Close reading and a thorough examination of technique will make your comparison stronger. Using the bullet points listed on the previous page will help you to approach your comparison in a focused and methodical way.

Once you are confident in analysing technique, you might find that the techniques used in your poems are linked with particular contexts. If you leapfrog from subject matter (what is happening in the text) to context (what is happening outside of the text) to make your links, you might find out **why** they have been written. But it is through your exploration of technique (the way both subject matter and context are communicated) that you will find out **how** they have been written.

Context

When you compare two or more poems or poetry collections from the same period, you can analyse whether contexts create similarities or differences in your texts.

- Are the subject matter, language, structure and form typical of the period from which they come? How? If not, what are they typical of?
- Are the poems typical of the period in the same ways or different ways?
- Which specific contexts do they reveal and/or share?
- Is there a literary context that influences the techniques? Does a particular social context influence what is written and how it is presented?

Poetry extracts and activities

Here are two poems written during the First World War: 'Suicide in the Trenches' (1918) by Siegfried Sassoon and 'Dulce et Decorum est' (1917) by Wilfred Owen.

During the First World War (1914–18), attitudes towards war changed and so did ways of writing about battle, death and loss. By the end of the war, Trench poetry had broken with two poetic traditions. First, subject matter and language that glorified war were often replaced with its horror, expressed through a realistic portrayal of suffering. Second, the dominance of traditional form was challenged. The Trench poets sought to write about experiences that could not always be contained in tight structures. They began to break traditional poetic structures into irregular chunks and patterns.

Did you know?

Carol Ann Duffy's tips on technique

Duffy has described her two approaches to writing a poem:

1. If it does not come easily, she puts it down (the inspirational aspect).

2. If she commits herself to a new poem, she might spend an entire day just choosing one verb (the perspiration aspect).

Think about it

The importance of verbs

To Carol Ann Duffy, verbs are the most important words in a poem because they carry:

- the actions and the events, as the doing words that tell you who does and feels what

- the mood, if they control the action.

Compare how your poets use verbs in two poems you are studying. Consider which words 'drive' the poems you choose. Which words seem to be 'alive' and make the poem reach you?

Examiner's tip

Technique in context

A sound grasp of the effects of technique provides you with textual evidence for your understanding of context. This attracts higher marks than a general overview of the world the text comes from.

Extract 1

'Suicide in the Trenches' (1918), Siegfried Sassoon

I knew a simple soldier boy
Who grinned at life in empty joy,
Slept soundly through the lonesome dark,
And whistled early with the lark.

In winter trenches, cowed and glum,
With crumps and lice and lack of rum,
He put a bullet through his brain.
No one spoke of him again.

You smug-faced crowds with kindling eye
Who cheer when soldier lads march by,
Sneak home and pray you'll never know
The hell where youth and laughter go.

p112, *Poems of the Great War 1914–1918* (Penguin, 1998)

Extract 2

'Dulce et Decorum est' (1917), Wilfred Owen

Bent double, like old beggars under sacks,
Knock-kneed, coughing like hags, we cursed through sludge,
Till on the haunting flares we turned our backs
And towards our distant rest began to trudge.
Men marched asleep. Many had lost their boots
But limped on, blood-shod. All went lame; all blind;
Drunk with fatigue; deaf even to the hoots
Of disappointed shells that dropped behind.

GAS! Gas! Quick, boys! – An ecstasy of fumbling,
Fitting the clumsy helmets just in time;
But someone still was yelling out and stumbling
And floundering like a man in fire or lime...
Dim, through the misty panes and thick green light
As under a green sea, I saw him drowning.

In all my dreams, before my helpless sight,
He plunges at me, guttering, choking, drowning.

If in some smothering dreams you too could pace
Behind the wagon that we flung him in,
And watch the white eyes writhing in his face,
His hanging face, like a devil's sick of sin;
If you could hear, at every jolt, the blood
Come gargling from the froth-corrupted lungs,
Obscene as cancer, bitter as the cud
Of vile, incurable sores on innocent tongues, –
My friend, you would not tell with such high zest
To children ardent for some desperate glory,
The old Lie: Dulce et decorum est
Pro patria mori.

p30, *Poems of the Great War 1914–1918* (Penguin, 1998)

Activity 1

Comparing Trench poetry

Compare and contrast the two Trench poems in Extracts 1 and 2.

AO 1

1. What is happening to the soldiers in the poems?

2. What are the messages about war?

AOs 1, 2 and 3

3. Compare how Owen and Sassoon use imagery (metaphors, similes and descriptions to imagine/create a scene) to present the soldiers and attitudes to war.

4. Compare how language is used to create the tone and mood. The verbs in the first verses have been highlighted as a starting point.

5. How do the poets address the reader? What role are you given?

AOs 3 and 4

6. How do you respond to these poems? You can focus on the last four lines of each if you like. Which do you prefer? Why?

7. Compare how these poems might have been received when they were written with their reception now.

AOs 1, 2, 3 and 4

8. If you are studying poetry from the First World War, **either** (i) compare one other poem you know with one or both of these two, **or** (ii) compare two other poems you know with each other. (Refer to questions 1–7.)

9. If you are studying poetry from or about any other war, choose two poems written within ten years of each other and answer questions 1–7.

Commentary on Activity 1

Subject matter

There are some clear similarities in the subject matter, such as the presentation of the soldiers as victims. A crucial difference in subject matter in Sassoon's poem is who killed the soldier. You might want to comment on whether Sassoon and Owen have similar or different messages about who is responsible for the death of soldiers, even when it is a case of suicide.

You might have felt that lost innocence was a powerful message in both of these poems. One response to the subject matter of these two poems is guilt at sending such young men to their deaths. Another response could be great pathos (sadness and pity) for the loss.

Technique

Owen's language is different from Sassoon's. Consider, for example, the level of description of the soldiers. Owen chooses different ways of describing a similar horror in the presentation of their deaths. Owen's language is more complex and intricate than Sassoon's. His use of hyphens suggests that the separate words are not enough to convey the emotion of the scene. Sassoon chooses simple language. His simplistic, almost childlike language reinforces his message about the lost innocence of soldiers who are barely more than boys. The form supports the language because it sounds like a nursery rhyme. In this way, the form carries the message that the soldier was too young and innocent to die.

Think about it

'Howls and hallelujahs'

Gillian Clarke, National Poet of Wales, believes the power of a poem comes from its 'howl' or 'hallelujah'. She says a poem must change how you felt before you read it, and move you through its expression of profound pain (howl) or uncontainable joy (hallelujah). Can you apply this idea to the Owen and Sassoon poems, or to two other poems that you are studying?

Context

The two poems demonstrate the use of traditional features, such as rhyme and rhythm. If you read the whole of Owen's poem, you can see that it does not have a completely regular pattern. The break with traditional form expresses how the war has broken and fragmented the soldiers, a generation of young men and society as a whole.

Now look at two poems from 1990: 'Intercity Lullaby' by Sheenagh Pugh and 'Translating the English, 1989' by Carol Ann Duffy.

Both these poems were written in the year that Margaret Thatcher stepped down as British Prime Minister and leader of the Conservative Party, after 11 years in power. Sheenagh Pugh evokes a contemporary anti-Thatcher reference in the last stanza of her poem when she says, 'I would make away the witch'. 'Witch' was the controversial label attached to Thatcher by people who felt that her policies damaged the economic and cultural survival of the British working class. When she died in 2013, the song 'Ding Dong! The Witch Is Dead' went to number 2 on the download charts. This protest shows how long Thatcher's legacy and reputation has lasted.

Carol Ann Duffy examines the Thatcher legacy in her collection *The Other Country* (1990), from where this poem comes. At a school reading of these poems, she told A Level students that the title came from her belief that Thatcher had made England into another country. She said that it was now the 'other' country – one she claimed not to recognise.

Extract 3

'Intercity Lullaby' (1990), Sheenagh Pugh

They're both what, nineteen? Their dark hair
flops: they've had a long day on the beer,
or the travel, sitting slumped in sleep,
each with his feet cradled in the other's lap.

Balulalow, beautiful tired boys,
and if I could, I would give you the choice
of where to spend your lives, and what to do:
you should not so be shuttled to and fro.

Newcastle United black and white
on their bags: they'll be in London tonight,
looking to find the streets paved with brass;
fairy tales are practical, nowadays.

Balow marras, balow canny lads,
and if I could, I would rebuild your trades
and let you play at home all seasons long
at doing what you liked, and being young.

Two stations back, they were talking about
the fair at Whitley Bay, while they ate
the food their mothers packed, just before
waving them off to look for their adventure.

Lullay innocents: lully, lully, lullay,
and if I could, I would make away
the witch: break spells, change the frog-prince's shape,
shut down the engine's noise to guard your sleep.

p24, *Selected Poems* (Seren, 1990)

Extract 4

'Translating the English, 1989' (1990), Carol Ann Duffy

'...and much of the poetry, alas, is lost in translation...'

Welcome to my country! We have here Edwina Currie
And the *Sun* newspaper. Much excitement.
Also the weather has been most improving
even in February. Daffodils. (Wordsworth. Up North.) If you like
Shakespeare or even Opera we have too the Black Market.
For two hundred quids we are talking *Les Miserables*,
nods being as good as winks. Don't eat the eggs.
Wheel-clamp. Dogs. Vagrants. A tour of our wonderful
capital city is not to be missed. The Fergie,
The Princess Di and the football hooligan, truly you will
like it here, Squire. Also we can be talking crack, smack
and Carling Black Label if we are so inclined. Don't
drink the H_2O. All very proud we now have
a green Prime Minister. What colour yours? Binbags.
You will be knowing of Charles Dickens and Terry Wogan
and Scotland. All this can be arranged for cash no questions.
Ireland not on. Fish and chips and the Official Secrets Act
second to none. Here we go. We are liking
a smashing good time like estate agents and *Neighbours*,
also *Brookside* for we are allowed four Channels.
How many you have? Last night of Proms. Andrew
Lloyd Webber, Jeffrey Archer. Plenty culture you will be agreeing.
Also history and buildings. The House of Lords. Docklands.
Many thrills and high interest rates for own good. Muggers.
Much lead in petrol. Filth. Rule Britannia and child abuse.
Electronic tagging, Boss, ten pints and plenty rape. Queen Mum.
Channel Tunnel. You get here fast no problem to my country
my country my country welcome welcome welcome.

p11, *The Other Country* (Anvil, 1990)

Pun a form of wordplay, where a word is given two or more separate and unconnected meanings.

Cliché an overused phrase or opinion based on a metaphor or simile that makes it seem like empty or meaningless language.

Irony Using language to mean the opposite of the normal meaning of the word, phrase, idea.

Activity 2

Comparing poetry from 1990

AO1

1. Identify the subject matter of each poem.

AOs 1 and 2

2. What is the role of each speaker in the poems?

AOs 1, 2 and 3

3. Compare how the speakers address the reader. Examine the different uses of the word 'you' and how this affects your response to the subject matter.

AOs 1, 2, 3 and 4

4. Compare the choice of titles. How does each word in each title point to the subject matter and any contexts you see in the poems?

5. Explore the use of techniques – for example, colloquialisms, accent and dialect, puns and clichés, verbs and verb tenses, and punctuation. Compare how this language use (i) presents the subject matter and (ii) reveals any contexts in the poems.

6. Examine the references to people and events from UK and Irish history and public life. Compare what the figures symbolise.

7. Compare the messages of these poems. What do you think are Duffy's and Pugh's messages about England and English society in 1989?

8. Which poem do you prefer? Why?

9. If you are studying poetry from this period, 1990 to the present, **either** (i) compare one other poem you know with one or both of these poems, **or** (ii) compare two other poems you know with each other. (Refer to questions 1–8.)

Commentary on Activity 2

Subject matter

Duffy begins with 'Welcome to my country!' (line 1) and finishes with 'welcome welcome welcome' (line 28). Some of the events or depictions of England and the English, however are presented as unwelcome aspects of English life or unwelcoming to 'outsiders'. The message is that not everyone is welcome to England in 1989.

Pugh echoes this concern about who and what is a welcome part of English life at the time, perhaps more explicitly than Duffy. She suggests changes in English life that she would welcome for her two 'canny lads', and lays the blame clearly at the politicians' feet.

Technique

Duffy's poem is written in the voice of a guide for tourists and visitors. There is irony in the use of 'welcome', strengthened by the repetition that begins and ends the poem. It is unclear how welcome the speaker is in his own society, and this contributes to the irony of the poem.

Pugh's poem has a different voice. It is written as if it were spoken by a mother or a sympathetic, caring adult. She encourages the reader to care for her subjects and suggests, like Duffy, that they are also unwelcome within their own society.

Pugh's poem has a tender mood and Duffy's is more humorous. Duffy uses satire in her observations of English life at the time. She uses free verse to present the social and political climate through a hotch-potch of nonsensical events and decisions. Pugh moves between the idea of a lullaby and a harsh social criticism of the politics of the time. Their two title words both support their ideas about what they think is missing from England at this time: 'Translating' and 'Lullaby'.

Contexts

The dialect and colloquial words, along with the facts and information about the time, will affect your understanding of the poems. You need some contextual knowledge of the contemporary cultures to grasp the ideas and messages in these poems.

Prose

To compare prose, novels and/or short stories, from the same period, consider how to find similarities, differences and a relevant focus, as you did with poetry.

Finding similarities and differences

Finding similarity in prose texts from the same period is a bit different from making these connections between poems or even poetry collections. The prose genre introduces and develops ideas and concerns more gradually, often in greater detail, with complex narratives built around the characters. The prose texts you are studying have characters that populate the setting and are central to the action and the plot. Your approach to prose needs to focus on those features, which is not necessary with poetry.

You can adopt the same process of starting with the subject matter, but you can begin with the text as a whole. (Dividing it into chapters and sections is useful for close reading activities, which we will do later in the chapter with a selection of extracts.) You need to get an overview of how the text fits together and works as a whole. The 'parts within the whole' become significant, and are crucially inter-related in a novel, and even a short story. Analysis of language is still important, but you will find it useful to start with the bigger picture of the narrative structure.

What to compare

Consider this method for finding similarities and differences in prose from the same genre and the same period.

Subject matter

Explore the subject matter of the prose texts to examine common elements.

- Identify what each prose text is about: the plot and sequence of events – the narrative element.

- Identify the characters. Examine how they feel, think, look, move, and so on – the descriptive element.

- Identify the place or landscapes of the characters – the setting/s. Are the settings imaginary or physical places? If there is a physical place, is it named? If it is an imaginary place, is it a fantasy? Are the settings concerned with what happens in the mind or human body? Is there a journey?

- What ideas, themes and concerns do the writers present to you?

> **Key terms**
>
> Satire ironic comedy which mocks and judges people, groups or organisations and their vices, such as corruption or greed.

> **Links**
>
> For more information on what you compare and how to apply the Assessment Objectives, see Chapter 1, pages 4–10.
>
> For more information on making connections between your texts, see Chapter 3, pages 16–19.

Narrators and viewpoints

- **First person**: a character narrates the world he or she experiences from a solely personal viewpoint.

- **Direct address**: a character narrates the story as if he or she is speaking to you, a listening audience. This can increase the intimacy between the individual reader and the narrator(s).

- **Third person**: the distance created by the viewpoint of an omniscient narrator (who is not a character) can (i) present an overview of more than one character, and (ii) intensify presentations of loneliness and isolation in individual characters.

Key terms

Naturalistic natural-sounding language, as it would actually be spoken, aloud or in someone's head.

Chronological narrative one that moves forward in time.

Flashback narrative one that initially looks back in time from the present to a moment in the past, then moves forwards again, towards the present moment.

Split narrative one that has at least two narrative strands running in any direction through time.

Think about it

TV, film and dramatic adaptations

Have your novels been adapted as films, serialised for TV or made into plays? Compare how you respond to the different genre/new versions. Compare how the adaptation changes the original narrative structure. Compare how those changes affect the presentation of the plots, characters and moods.

Use these questions to compare what the prose texts are about and the settings of their subject matter. You can then tackle comparisons of technique.

Technique

Explore **how** the subject matter of the prose texts is presented to the reader.

Viewpoint

- Identify the narrative viewpoints. Who tells the story? Is there a third-person (omniscient) narrator or a first-person narrator, or both? Are there multiple first-person narrators?

- What relationships are any narrators attempting to create with you? Do they speak to you directly?

- Are you invited to observe a third party and/or given intimate details about the narrators themselves?

- Who created that – the narrators or the writers? What is the difference between these two viewpoints?

Language

- What types of language are being used? For example, is it formal or naturalistic, colloquial or slang?

- How does the type of language affect the presentation of subject matter?

- How is dialogue used to present the characters, their relationships and their importance in the plot?

Plots and narrative structures

- There are three significant ways to structure storylines in your prose texts: chronological narrative, flashback narrative and split narrative.

- Which structures do your texts use?

- How do they support the presentation of the plot and characters?

- How is the structure used to present themes, ideas and messages?

Subgenre

Subgenre is both a technique (AO2) and a literary context (AO4).

- Is subgenre useful when comparing prose texts?

- Does it link to the narrative viewpoints and use of narrators?

Tackling technique

You can compare the effects of the choices that your novelists make, and how those choices influence the relationship between the reader and the texts. The structure partly controls how you make meaning from text: the ways in which the plots, any subplots, themes, ideas, characters and settings unfold for you in a particular sequence. An examination of the narrative structure of whole prose texts can also help you to develop an analysis of other techniques that are used. For example, narrative structure is linked to narrative viewpoint – the teller is delivering the tale to you bit by bit.

If you are comparing novels from the same subgenre, see if they favour a particular structure. For example, many prose texts described as being from a Gothic subgenre use a flashback structure. Some Gothic novels that feature ghosts, malevolent spirits and links with the underworld or supernatural use this structure to look back to an innocent, less knowing past, recalling a time before the evil took hold of the characters or became embedded in the setting. The narrator might be wistfully or fearfully recalling events to show the reader how this point in the plot has been reached. The narrator could speak in direct address to draw you in. This approach takes the following form: 'Dear reader, you see, it happened like this… If only I could have seen before what I tell you now…' *Frankenstein* (1818) and *Wuthering Heights* (1847) are two examples of this technique. You can also see how the structure of *Wuthering Heights* is complicated beyond a basic flashback structure and differs from *Frankenstein* in the delivery of its ideas and messages as a result.

A subgenre can use any narrative structure, such as the bildungsroman. A bildungsroman tends to favour a first-person narrator as an ideal vehicle to carry this type of tale: for example, *To Kill a Mockingbird* (1960) by Harper Lee, *The Catcher in the Rye* (1951) by J.D. Salinger and *David Copperfield* (1850) by Charles Dickens. If you are comparing bildungsromans, see if and how first-person narrators are used.

> ### Did you know?
>
> **Bildungsroman**
> Typically, a novel of this type narrates the fortunes of a young hero or heroine, who 'comes of age' through personal experience and struggle in his or her journey from childhood to adulthood. It can also be described as a 'rite of passage', if a particular experience leads to permanent changes in the character's life.

Context

When you compare two or more prose texts from the same period, you can analyse whether contexts create similarities or differences in your texts.

- Identify the period. Is the choice of structure due to the time of composition? For example, if you compare late 20th-century prose texts, they often have a different structure to their 18th- or 19th-century counterparts.
- Are the subject matters, language, forms and subgenres typical of the period from which they come? How? If not, what are they typical of?
- Examine the literary contexts and cultural movements that influence your texts.

Prose extracts and activities

Compare two extracts of novels written in the same period, around the millennium, to see how they tell their stories: *The Kite Runner* (2003) by Khaled Hosseini and *Spies* (2002) by Michael Frayn.

This first extract comes from the final pages of *The Kite Runner,* where the narrator, Amir, is flying a kite with Sohrab, the young son of his closest childhood friend, Hassan. Amir and Sohrab are from Kabul in Afghanistan, but as a result of the war in Afghanistan now live together in the San Francisco area of the US. Hassan was killed in Afghanistan, along with Sohrab's mother. The boy is traumatised by his wartime experiences and has stopped speaking. Amir and Hassan flew kites together as boys, when Hassan would run to catch the defeated kites of their opponents for Amir.

Extract 5

The Kite Runner (2003), Khaled Hosseini

'Did I ever tell you your father was the best kite runner in Wazir Akbar Khan? Maybe all of Kabul?' I said, knotting the loose end of the spool *tar* to the string loop tied to the center spar. 'How jealous he made the neighbourhood kids. He'd run kites and never look up at the sky, and people used to say he was chasing the kite's shadow. But they didn't know him like I did. Your father wasn't chasing any shadows. He just … knew.'

Another half-dozen kites had taken flight. People had started to gather in clumps, teacups in hand, eyes glued to the sky.

'Do you want to help me fly this?' I said.

Sohrab's gaze bounced from the kite to me. Back to the sky.

'Okay.' I shrugged. 'Looks like I'll have to fly it *tanhaii*.' Solo.

I balanced the spool in my left hand and fed about three feet of *tar*. The yellow kite dangled at the end of it, just above the wet grass. 'Last chance,' I said. But Sohrab was looking at a pair of kites tangling high above the trees.

'All right. Here I go.' I took off running, my sneakers splashing rainwater from puddles, the hand clutching the kite end of the string held high above my head. It had been so long, so many years since I'd done this, and I wondered if I'd make a spectacle of myself. I let the spool roll in my left hand as I ran, felt the string cut my right hand again as it fed through. The kite was lifting behind my shoulder now, lifting, wheeling, and I ran harder. The spool spun faster and the glass string tore another gash in my right palm. I stopped and turned. Looked up. Smiled. High above my kite was tilting side to side like a pendulum, making that old paper-bird-flapping-its-wings sound I had always associated with winter mornings in Kabul. I hadn't flown a kite in a quarter of a century, but suddenly I was twelve again and all the old instincts came rushing back.

I felt a presence next to me and looked down. It was Sohrab. Hands dug deep in the pockets of his raincoat. He had followed me. 'Do you want to try?' I asked. He said nothing. But when I held the string out for him, his hand lifted from his pocket. Hesitated. Took the string. My heart quickened as I spun the spool to gather the loose string. We stood quietly side by side. Necks bent up.

Around us, kids chased each other, slid on the grass. Someone was playing an old Hindi movie soundtrack now. A line of elderly men were praying afternoon *namaz* on a plastic sheet spread on the ground. The air smelled of wet grass, smoke, and grilled meat. I wished time would stand still.

Then I saw we had company. A green kite was closing in. I traced the string to a kid standing about thirty yards from us. He had a crew cut and a T-shirt that read THE ROCK RULES. He saw me looking at him and smiled. Waved. I waved back.

Sohrab was handing the string back to me.

'Are you sure?' I said, taking it.

He took the spool from me.

'Okay,' I said. 'Let's give him a *sabagh*, teach him a lesson, nay?' I glanced over at him. The glassy, vacant look in his eyes was gone. His gaze flitted between our kite and the green one. His face was a little flushed, his eyes suddenly alert. Awake. Alive. I wondered when I had forgotten that, despite everything, he was still just a child.

The green kite was making its move. 'Let's wait,' I said. 'We'll let him get a little closer.' It dipped twice and crept towards us. 'Come on. Come to me,' I said. The green kite drew closer yet, now rising a little above us, unaware of the trap I'd set for it. 'Watch, Sohrab. I'm going to show you one of your father's favourite tricks, the old lift-and-dive.'

…

I did it perfectly. After all these years. The old lift-and-dive trap. I loosened my grip and tugged on the string, dipping and dodging the green kite. A series of quick sidearm jerks and our kite shot up counter-clockwise, in a half circle. Suddenly I was on top. The green kite was scrambling now, panic-stricken. But it was too late. I'd already slipped him Hassan's trick. I pulled hard and our kite plummeted. I could almost feel our string sawing his. Almost heard the snap.

Then, just like that, the green kite was spinning and wheeling out of control.

Behind us, people cheered. Whistles and applause broke out. I was panting. The last time I had felt a rush like this was that day in the winter of 1975, just after I had cut the last kite, when I spotted Baba* on our rooftop, clapping, beaming.

I looked down at Sohrab. One corner of his mouth had curled up just so.

A smile.

Lopsided.

Hardly there.

But there.

Behind us, kids were scampering, and a melee of screaming kite runners was chasing the loose kite drifting high above the trees. I blinked and the smile was gone. But it had been there. I had seen it.

'Do you want me to run that kite for you?'

*[Baba – father]

pp321–3, *The Kite Runner* (Bloomsbury, 2011 edn [2003])

This extract comes from the final pages of the novel, *Spies,* where the narrator, Stephen Wheatley recalls and reveals the secrets of his childhood in a British town during the Second World War.

Extract 6
Spies (2002), Michael Frayn

There were many things that Keith had been wrong about, I realised gradually as life went on. But about one thing, and one quite surprising thing, he'd been right, though it took me several years to recognise it. There was a German spy in the Close that summer. It wasn't his mother – it was me.

Everything is as it was; and everything has changed. Stephen Wheatley has become this old man, treading slowly and warily in the footsteps of his former self, and the name of this old man is Stefan Weitzler. That undersized observer in the privet, spying on the comings and goings of the street, has reverted to the name under which he was registered in the peaceful green district of the great German city where he was born.

I was reborn as Stephen when my parents left Germany in 1935. My mother was English anyway, and she'd always spoken English to us at home, but now my father became more English still, and we all turned into Wheatleys. She died at the beginning of the 1960s, and when my father followed her less than a year later I felt a great restlessness stirring in me – the converse of that same restlessness that's brought me back now to the Close. It's the longing to be elsewhere that in Germany we call *Fernweh*, which is in my case also *Heimweh*, a longing to be home – the terrible pull of opposites that torments the displaced everywhere.

…

Actually there were *two* German spies in the Close, now I come to think about it – and the other one was a serious and dedicated professional.

I once tried to gain a little credit with Keith by claiming that my father was a German spy. Well, so he was, I discovered later. At any rate he was a German, and he had some kind of job in economic intelligence, though he was on the British side, not the German. This was why he came back when he did from that mysterious 'business trip' of his to the North. They gave him an early release from his internment as an enemy alien in the Isle of Man because they needed his knowledge of the German optical industry, and his ability to understand decrypts relating to it. Someone who'd worked on the history of the Allied bombing campaign once told me that if it hadn't have been for the work of his department, the Germans would have been better supplied with gunsights, and Uncle Peter and his colleagues would have had a harder time still with German anti-aircraft defences.

I suppose I've got more and more like my father as I've got older. I hear myself saying the same irritatingly eccentric things that he used to say, that I never realised at the time were simply plain, ordinary German. I'd look into my son's bedroom when he was a child and tell him off for the frightful *Kuddelmuddel*, and when he tried to offer some excuse I'd snap that it was nonsense, just as my father would have done: *Schnickschnack*!

Yes, we were the Germans, in a country at war with them, and no-one ever knew it. No one except me overheard the pleas of desperate fellow-refugees who came to my father for help. No one else guessed what language they were speaking together. We were also the Juice, in a juiceless district (the mysterious dark strangers at Trewinnick turned out to be Orthodox Greeks) and no one ever knew that, either.

pp228–9, 230–31, *Spies* (Faber, 2003 edn [2002])

Activity 3

Comparing novel endings
AO1

1. What is happening in each extract?

2. Identify any themes of the novels that you can from reading these extracts.

AOs 1 and 2
The novels these extracts come from have a flashback structure.

3. Examine how each ending:

- concludes the plot

- presents the central characters

- presents the final mood

- presents the passage of time.

AOs 1, 2 and 3

4. Examine the balance between the narrative and descriptive elements of each extract. Compare which parts bring you into the present moments of the text and which parts take you to the past.

AOs 1, 2, 3 and 4
These novels are examples of bildungsroman.

5. Examine how the narrators try to understand important events and experiences from the past.

6. Compare the presentation of their reflections and their effects on the mood/s of the extracts.

7. How do the writers use individual words from languages other than English? Compare the effects of these words on each novel ending.

8. How do you respond to these extracts? Which do you prefer? Why?

9. If you are studying a novel written after 1990 with a flashback structure and/or a bildungsroman subgenre and/or a first-person narrator recalling their childhood and/or themes of war and conflict, family relationships, displacement and loss, compare the ending with one or both of these novels.

10. Use this activity to compare the endings of two novels from the same period if they share a flashback structure and/or a bildungsroman subgenre and/or a first-person narrator recalling their childhood.

Commentary on Activity 3
Technique
Comparing literary features and parts of your novels or short stories supports your analysis of the whole texts. A comparison of their use of language and structure through close reading of extracts is vital to support your arguments. For example, the flashback structures in these two extracts is closely interwoven with the subject matter.

Subject matter
Message

The methods of telling the story can also tell you about the messages of the novels. These two novels present a tale of how childhood innocence is lost too soon in wartime. At the same time, they both show how war remains separate from the private world of childhood innocence. You grasp the message – can childhood innocence survive the worldliness and corruption of a society at war? – partly through their use of narrative structure. The adult character tells you how they became an adult through the release of the significant details of their childhood memories. You might have found that the big picture linking the narratives, war, is not always the central element. Relationships with boyhood friends and parents might be more significant in these examples.

Theme

Comparing messages leads you to compare themes. Novels with messages about childhood innocence in wartime have universal themes about war. They also concern the small, detailed world of children, with their different scale of meaningful events and ways of seeing them.

Drama

To compare drama from the same period, consider how to find similarities, differences and a relevant focus, as you did with the poetry and prose genres.

Finding similarities and differences

Finding similarities and differences in the drama genre requires you to examine texts that are designed to be performed. Drama does share the narrative element of prose and some types of poetry. Like prose, plays have a story to tell through their characters, in a structured sequence of actions and events. Events can be structured in the same ways as novels: chronologically, in flashback and in split narratives. Like poetry, some plays are traditionally written in verse. Like the poetic form of a dramatic monologue, the drama genre can include long monologues designed to develop a relationship with the live audience.

However, drama is an action-propelled genre. Description, or scene-setting, is achieved through:

- dialogue, which can establish the time and place
- stage directions, which are cues for a director.

A play is what we call the **realisable text**. Approaches to performance can differ because drama is the genre that has an 'unfinished' text. The script is there to guide the play's transformation from the page to the stage. The possibilities of interpretation can mean a wide range of ways of visualising the play in performance. You are not only comparing your plays as written texts but also how they can be experienced.

Identify the subgenres of the plays you are comparing, which we consider below. Pay attention to how your plays use language as the action and description is all conveyed through characters talking, either to each other or to you in the audience.

What to compare

Consider this method for finding similarities and differences in drama from the same genre and the same period.

Subject matter

Explore the subject matter of the dramas to examine common elements.

- Identify what each play text is about: the plot, any subplots and sequence of events.

> ## Remember
>
> ### Genre conventions of drama
>
> - A **play** is narrative in action, structured into acts and scenes, where actors enact the lines of the script.
>
> - **Stage directions describe and guide** the physical setting and staging, the appearance and behaviour of characters, and background information for directors, actors and technicians to realise the script.
>
> - **Characters speak dialogue** (or conversation) with others, a **monologue** by themselves, a **soliloquy** to the audience when alone on the stage, or an **aside** directly to the audience to hide something from other characters on stage.

> ## Key term
>
> **Realisable text** one which can be brought to life with actors, the drama genre.

Stylised a style that is artificial rather than realistic.

Sympathy emotional identification with a character's situation.

Tragi-comedy a play with tragic beginnings that ends in comedy.

Comic relief a comic or funny episode in a tragedy play that lessens the effects or reflects the ideas of the main tragic plot.

Tragic hero(ine) a flawed hero(ine) who makes mistakes and causes the downfall of several characters, along with him- or herself.

Resolution the dramatic outcome in which all aspects of the plot, structure, themes and character relationships are concluded.

Did you know?

Styles of tragedy in the 20th century

The American playwrights Arthur Miller and Tennessee Williams wrote particular styles of tragedy that were instrumental in the evolution of the genre during the 20th century.

- They made tragic heroes of common men (for example, Miller's Willy Loman in *Death of a Salesman*) and women (for example, Williams' Blanche Dubois in *A Streetcar Named Desire*), rather than people of great fortune (for example, the king in Shakespeare's *King Lear*).
- They created endings that delivered symbolic death: the death of a way of life or a relationship, the loss of individual status or even sanity, the end of their social, economic and political survival.

- Identify the characters. Examine how they feel, think, look, talk to each other and the audience.
- Identify the place or landscapes of the characters: setting/s. Is setting important in the plays? Are the settings imaginary or physical places? If there is a physical place, is it named? If it is an imaginary place, is it a fantasy? Are the settings concerned with what happens in the mind or human body? Is there a journey?
- What ideas, themes and concerns do the dramatists present to you?

Use these questions to compare what the drama texts are about and the settings for their subject matter. You can then tackle comparisons of technique.

Technique

Language

- Identify ways in which the characters talk to each other and the audience. How do they use language to create these relationships?
- Identify if the dramatic language is naturalistic or stylised. Does it sound like ordinary speech? Formal speech? Poetry? Declamation?
- Compare how the performance elements of language are used: for example, silence, whispering, pauses, interruption and overlapping. How does the text alert you to these features?

Subgenre

- Subgenre is both a technique (AO2) and a literary context (AO4). Look at dramatic endings. How is the plot concluded? What are the outcomes for its characters?
- Is the mood happy or grave, or both?
- Where is your sympathy directed?

Tackling technique

To compare the significance of dramatic subgenres, you need to know the conventions of the subgenres that influence or label your plays. Historically, drama is broadly divided into the subgenres of tragedy and comedy. Tragi-comedy developed as a hybrid of the two. Comic relief offers humour within tragedy, and satire offers grim suffering and punishment in a comedy. You need to know the relevant dramatic conventions in order to compare drama from these traditions.

Styles of tragedy and comedy have developed and evolved into many complex varieties, with more flexible features and outcomes. By the 20th century, these broad categories had been challenged. By the end of the 20th century, the distinct dramatic subgenres of tragedy and comedy have been changed. It is now more difficult to identify the subgenre of a play by its subject matter, character types (such as tragic heroes), mood, settings and endings (resolutions). Categories of comedy and tragedy are no longer adequate ways to analyse many of our modern plays.

Late 20th-century hybrid dramatic subgenres typically have an ending 'without an answer'. This feature is the opposite of the recognised features of traditional forms. As a result, comparing contemporary plays is complex. It is more useful to talk about tragic and comic elements in drama in many of the plays you might compare.

Contexts

When you compare two or more dramas from the same period, you can analyse whether contexts create similarities or differences in your texts.

- Examine the literary contexts of your plays. How important are they to any subgenres you have identified? For example, specific subgenres may be identified with a period in time, such as early 17th-century Jacobean revenge tragedy, late 17th-century Restoration comedy, post-war Theatre of the Absurd and 1960s kitchen-sink realist dramas.

- How and to what effect do your plays use the styles of the subgenre from the period?

- How do the political and social contexts (the world outside of the text) influence the way the dramatists voice their concerns and ideas within the texts?

Drama extracts and activities

We are going to consider two examples of plays from the Elizabethan and Jacobean era, written during the English Renaissance: the Elizabethan tragedy of *Doctor Faustus* (1594) by Christopher Marlowe and the Jacobean revenge tragedy of *The White Devil* (1609–12) by John Webster.

Extract 7 is from the middle of the *The White Devil*. Vittoria is a noblewoman on trial for her alleged part in the murder of her husband. However, as the trial progresses, some critics argue that she is on trial for something else: being a strong woman who stands up to her accusers and lawyers, including Monticelso. Her lover, the powerful Duke Brachiano, actually committed the murder, but never stands trial.

Extract 7

The White Devil (1609–12), John Webster

MONTICELSO
And look upon this creature was his wife.
She comes not like a widow: she comes armed
With scorn and impudence. Is this a mourning habit?
VITTORIA
Had I foreknown his death as you suggest,
I would have bespoke my mourning.
MONTICELSO   O you are cunning.
VITTORIA
You shame your wit and judgement
To call it so. What, is my just defence
By him that is my judge called impudence?
Let me appeal then from this Christian court
To the uncivil Tartar.
MONTICELSO   See my lords,
She scandals our proceedings.
VITTORIA [*Kneeling*]   Humbly thus,
Thus low, to the most worthy and respected
Lieger ambassadors, my modesty
And womanhood I tender; but withal
So entangled in a cursed accusation
That my defence, of force, like Perseus
Must personate masculine virtue to the point.
Find me but guilty, sever head from body:

We'll part good friends: I scorn to hold my life
At yours or any man's entreaty, sir.
ENGLISH AMBASSADOR
She hath a brave spirit.
MONTICELSO
Well, well, such counterfeit jewels
Make true ones oft suspected.
VITTORIA   You are deceived.
For know that all your strict combined heads,
Which strike against this mine of diamonds,
Shall prove but glassen hammers, they shall break;
These are but feigned shadows of my evils.
Terrify babes, my lord, with painted devils,
I am past such needless palsy, for your names
Of Whore and Murd'ress, they proceed from you,
As if a man should spit against the wind,
The filth returns in's face.

Act 3, Scene 2, Lines 120–150, *The White Devil* (1609–12)

Extract 8 is from the ending of *Doctor Faustus*. Faustus, the tragic hero of the play, fulfils his part of the bargain with the Devil by signing over his soul in exchange for 24 years of magic powers on earth. Here, he awaits his fate alone before descending into Hell.

Extract 8

Doctor Faustus (1594), Christopher Marlowe

FAUSTUS
Let Faustus live in hell a thousand years,
A hundred thousand, and at last be saved.
No end is limited to damned souls.
Why wert thou not a creature wanting soul?
Or why is this immortal that thou hast?
O, Pythagoras' metempsychosis, were that true,
This soul should fly from me and I be changed
Into some brutish beast.
All beasts are happy, for, when they die,
Their souls are soon dissolved in elements;
But mine must live still to be plagued in hell.
Curst be the parents that engendered me!

No, Faustus, curse thyself. Curse Lucifer,
That hath deprived thee of the joys of heaven.
        The clock strikes twelve
It strikes, it strikes! Now, body, turn to air,
Or Lucifer will bear thee quick to hell.
O soul, be changed into small waterdrops,
And fall into the ocean, ne'er be found!
Thunder, and enter the Devils
O, mercy, heaven, look not so fierce on me!
Adders and serpents, let me breathe a while!
Ugly hell, gape not. Come not, Lucifer!
I'll burn my books. O, Mephistopheles!
        Exeunt

Act 5, Scene 2, Lines 163–185, *Doctor Faustus*, B-text (1594)

Activity 4

Comparing pre-1770 tragedy
AOs 1 and 3
These two extracts come from the point in each play when Vittoria and Faustus face judgement.

1. Identify what you think is happening at these points.

2. Compare the subject matter in the passages.

3. What do you think are the messages in these extracts?

AOs 2 and 3
4. Compare the use of mood and tone in the extracts.

5. Examine the use of rhetorical questioning, exclamation and any line-sharing. How do these techniques:

   (i) create the pace of the scenes

   (ii) affect an audience?

AOs 1, 2 and 3
6. Compare how emotive words, repetition and internal rhyming of words within the lines are used to deliver the messages.

7. Consider the use of commands by Marlowe and the statements by Webster. How do they contribute to the subject matter and mood? How do the different types of questioning work in the two texts?

8. How are the characters presented in these extracts? Consider Vittoria's relationship with the court, in particular Monticelso, and how the audience might see Faustus.

9. What do you think happens to Faustus and Vittoria? Why?

AOs 1, 2, 3 and 4
10. Compare how description and imagery are used to create a mood that is typical of tragedy from this era and violent drama with Gothic elements.

11. How does your grasp of any contexts help you to understand these extracts?

12. If you are studying either or both of these plays, compare these extracts with an episode of another pre-1770 tragedy you know, where justice or judgement is being presented. Use the questions above as a guide to address the Assessment Objectives in your answer.

Commentary on Activity 4
Subject matter
In both extracts, a main character faces their moment of judgement. Where Vittoria faces a court, Faustus faces the devil himself. Both experience a trial and both are already condemned, but in different ways. Faustus's judgement is eternal; Vittoria's is earthly.

Webster's message is that the devil can come disguised as innocence, symbolised by the colour white. You have to decide, like a court, whether Vittoria is the white devil or if that title belongs to another character. Marlowe's message is that Faustus is damned from the start, entirely by himself and his own actions.

Technique

The title *The White Devil* encourages you to see the devil everywhere and in everyone. The presentation of character in this scene makes it hard to decide who it is. You might sympathise with Vittoria as a scapegoat for the prejudices of the men in the court. She is repeatedly named as a 'whore', even though that is not the reason she is on trial. Sympathy for Faustus is complex. He does not repent, so the contemporary audience would see his fate as just. Faustus names himself simply as 'Faustus', but the language is equally vulgar as that used by Webster. He fears that he 'be changed / Into some brutish beast.'

Contexts

Both these plays are tragedies, and both characters meet their fate and die as part of the corruption they have entered and created. In Marlowe's play, it is the tragedy of Faustus alone and is typical of Elizabethan and Jacobean tragedies with a main **protagonist**, a tragic hero. It is concerned with the Renaissance idea of man's thirst for knowledge and change against the tension of the dominant religious ideas of the time. Webster's play is a Jacobean revenge tragedy, but he is also concerned with the social and political position of women. He challenges the religious ideology and institutions of the time to suggest that the hierarchy itself is corrupt, not just individuals within his society. The gruesome language and dark mood contribute to Gothic elements in both of the plays.

> **Key term**
>
> **Protagonist** a central character, whose fortunes in the plot are important throughout the play.

Summary

This chapter has introduced you to comparing texts from the same genre and period. You should now be able to identify similarities and differences and do a comparative analysis of a range of same-period examples of:

- poetry
- prose
- drama.

5   Same genre, different period

Identifying similarities and differences

When you compare texts from the same genre, you can analyse how they might share technical features of their genre. When those texts are written at different times, you can see how each period uses the same genre to explore specific techniques that were popular in their time. You can also compare how writers use the same genre across time to respond to the types of subject matter and ideas that are important to their society and culture.

This can be more challenging than the connections you made in Chapter 4. However, because you are starting with the same text type or genre, you can still uncover several connections across each of the Assessment Objectives.

To compare the same genre over time, you should examine how the forms can be connected. They might share a subgenre. The subgenre might have been unchanged, adapted or even transformed, to reflect the concerns of the later period and the contexts in which the writer produced the later texts.

If you find that the forms have more differences than similarities, leave them until you have found more accessible ways to compare your texts. Look at any links between language use. Language in literary texts will have changed across time, but you might find some shared features of language use.

Subject matter can provide useful comparisons across time. Even when the worlds outside of the texts you compare are very different, your texts might explore shared universal themes, such as justice or loss of a loved one.

Even though the writers have chosen the same genre and subject matter to communicate their ideas and concerns, they are writing at different periods in time. This means that, inevitably, the texts will be influenced by different contexts and events.

Their historical, political, social and cultural contexts will contrast. Their literary contexts may also differ. However, later writers can draw on an earlier era for inspiration or use older styles as a model for their own writing. If a society or culture wants to embody the ideals of an earlier time, this ambition is reflected in its cultural practices and output, which include literature. If a writer is interested in the ways that an earlier writer used the genre and its features, he or she might adopt or develop the styles of the earlier tradition.

Subject matter

As you know, subject matter (AO1) covers the plots, characters, themes, messages and concerns.

- Can you compare what your texts are about? Do they share any ideas and concerns? Do they have common universal themes?
- Can you compare characters and/or speakers and their relationships, behaviour, experiences, emotions and observations?

Chapter aims

In this chapter we will look at how to compare texts from the same genre but from different periods. We will consider:

- poetry
- prose
- drama.

Links

For more information on what to compare and how to apply the Assessment Objectives, see Chapter 1, pages 4–10.

For more information on making connections between your texts, see Chapter 3, pages 16–19.

Examiner's tip

Struggling to compare your texts?

If AO1 proves too difficult to compare, perhaps your texts are not well chosen. If this is coursework, change them. If it is an exam where you have some choice over which poems or episodes and examples you use, think carefully about whether yours will work together.

- Can you compare the settings – places in the physical world, such as nature or a house, unnamed or named, real or imaginary?

Use these questions to help you explore how the subject matter is presented: for example, the structure, characterisation, tone, mood and setting. This will lead you to explore the techniques (AO2) used in your text.

Techniques

Form

- Do your same-genre texts share a similar form – for example, the sonnet, the bildungsroman or the romantic comedy?
- Do your texts use form in the same ways? For example, there are several ways to structure a sonnet, a bildungsroman and a romantic comedy, depending on the messages and the contexts that influence your writers.
- Do your texts use the same form to explore similar subject matter – for example, a sonnet to explore ideas about love, a bildungsroman to chart the suffering of a child orphaned by war or poverty, a romantic comedy to comment on unfaithful lovers in sexual relationships?
- Do your texts use a different form to explore similar subject matter? And so on.

Use these questions to help you to compare how the form is used to convey the meaning of the text and how it reveals the contexts (AO4) that influence the text.

Comparing form across time

You can consider how to compare form across time with the example of a poetic form, the sonnet. The sonnet was popularised in England during the Elizabethan era, not least by Shakespeare, who published a collection of 154 sonnets in 1609 which we still study today. As a traditional form, the sonnet has undergone many tweaks and changes to its structure. However, it still has a recognisable structure within a recognisable form: 14 lines of iambic pentameter which use rhyme, and a stanza structure that ends with a rhyming couplet. Modern sonnets continue to use the form for a debate on matters of romantic love, or to address philosophical matters by resolving a question posed at the start.

In the 21st century, sonnets are still popular. Carol Ann Duffy is a prolific sonneteer – for example, 'Prayer' (1993) from *Mean Time*. You can also find poems that are labelled as sonnets that you might think are nothing like sonnets and cannot be compared as such – for example, the 12 prose sonnets by Patience Agbabi in her collection *Bloodshot Monochrome* (2008). These are formatted as a sequence of magazine problem pages, with a question-and-answer structure across two stanzas. If you study them, you can see how much their structure and subject matter have in common with Shakespearean sonnets. They also work as intertextual debates between Agbabi's concerns about writing poetry now and the concerns of sonneteers across 500 years.

You can also consider prose forms such as the early 18th-century subgenre of the **epistolary novel**. For example with its episodes of a chronological narrative, still appeals to writers and readers today. Writers in the 19th century developed the epistolary form to include the use of ship's logs, diary entries, and so on. This can be seen in novels with Gothic elements, such as

Key term

Epistolary novel where the novel is written as a series of letters to carry the chronological narrative.

Frankenstein and *Dracula.* The 20th-century novel *The Color Purple* (1982) by Alice Walker is a modern example of the epistolary form.

Structure

- Can you compare ways in which your same-genre texts sequence their events and ideas?
- Can you compare how the structure affects the mood – for example, to build tension or create suspense?
- Can you compare how the structure is used to present narrative or poetic viewpoints?
- Can you compare how the structure is used to present the passage of time in your texts?

Use these questions to help you to compare how the structure is used to convey the meaning of the text, and how it reveals the contexts (AO4) that influence the text.

Comparing structure across time

You can consider how to compare structure across time by looking at the narrative structure of a text. Even though prose texts change over time, in many of the novels you study you will find that there is still a story, presented as a plot driven by a narrative structure. The chronological narrative structure, for example, became popular in the 18th century. It has since been adapted into more complex narrative structures, used when writers want to tell several stories at once and to move across time in nonlinear ways. Even such time-travelling methods have their roots in a time-driven structure that takes its name from something in which the passage of time is vital: 'chronological' – that is, events ordered by the time in which they take place.

Language

- What types of language are being used – for example, is it formal, colloquial or slang?
- How does the type of language affect the presentation of the subject matter?
- Do the writers use types of language that reflect the period they are writing in?

Use these questions to help you to compare how language is used to convey meaning of the text and how it reveals the contexts (AO4) that influence the text.

Comparing language across time

You can consider how to compare language across time with the example of novels from the 19th and 20th centuries. Consider three Gothic novels – *Wuthering Heights* (1847) by Emily Brontë, *Frankenstein* (1818) by Mary Shelley and *Dracula* (1897) by Bram Stoker – all written in the 19th century. If you compare the language, you will find, not surprisingly, that there are some similarities in the style, tone, viewpoint and reader address. However, now compare the dialogue and voices of characters from very different novels: *Wuthering Heights* and a novel from more than a century later, such as *The Color Purple* (1982) by Alice Walker. Brontë's character of the working-class servant Joseph speaks in a Yorkshire dialect that is typical of his class, location and period. Walker's central character Celie, a young black girl from the rural south of the US, also speaks in dialect. This comparison shows ways in which Celie and Joseph are presented with some similarities in their social status and even their life chances. The key to the comparison is in the language they speak. Their dialect tells the reader something about their characters and offers a realistic presentation of people in hardship. Celie is a central character and Joseph is a minor character. She is presented in detail; he is a sketch, even a stock character. She is presented with great sadness to encourage sympathy; he is possibly a figure of fun for comic relief within the story of Cathy and Heathcliff. These are the differences that you can uncover when you analyse how the characters are connected by the way they speak.

Literary traditions

A literary tradition is an accepted use of particular features that are considered to be an important aspect of a particular genre and/or period. For example, we have the literary tradition of love poetry that uses the sonnet form – developed by Shakespeare and still used today. We have the literary tradition of tragedy that depicts suffering and death using drama – popular since classical Greece and at its height in the Elizabethan era. We have a literary tradition of Victorian novels that use some principles of tragedy, such as a tragic hero(ine) who dies at the end, as in *Tess of the d'Urbervilles* (1891) by Thomas Hardy. Recognition of literary tradition enables us to place texts within a specific tradition across time. It allows us to relate the new to what has gone before.

Applying a literary tradition to a genre

Consider how literary tradition works in the drama genre. One example is Shakespeare, whose plays reflect Greek and Roman classical influences. You might be encouraged to make these connections if you compare, for example, Shakespeare's tragedy *King Lear* (1608) and *Oedipus Rex* (429 BC) by the Greek tragedian, Sophocles. It was not until the 20th century that the Greek-influenced traditional subgenres of drama such as tragedy and comedy began to alter radically.

After the First World War, playwrights, such as Sean O'Casey, Tennessee Williams and Arthur Miller, began to develop different models or types of tragedy. However, as a result of cultural and literary developments after the Second World War and their impact on drama, by the late 20th century, the fluid mixing of hybrid subgenres transformed drama beyond the recognisable boundaries and conventions of the tragedy and comedy subgenres.

This brief trace of a few thousand years of the literary heritage in Western drama shows that times change, but people often still find a connection with what their ancestors have written. Consequently, despite different periods and many differing contexts, where one society or world seems to speak to another, you can find that the literary contexts from the earlier period influence those from the later period in the texts you compare. This can provide you with fruitful connections to analyse. The differences in how the forms and themes are used will arise from the departures from tradition and the reasons for these. You can uncover these reasons from your analysis of the similarities first.

Let us now turn to how you can compare texts of each genre across different periods.

Did you know?

Literary tradition: an example

The English Renaissance of the 16th century (itself developing as part of the spread of the European Renaissance of the 14th and 15th centuries) is an attempt to embrace the classical ideas of Ancient Greece and Rome. The impact of this classical rebirth of philosophical ideas, and its relationship with literary forms, produced drama from the Elizabethan and Jacobean eras (1590–1640) that has been called a Golden Age.

Poetry

In the last chapter, you looked at how to make connections between pairs of poems that are both from the 20th century. Next, you can compare two pairs of poems; each pair compares a poem from the 21st century with a poem from an earlier century. See how this affects the ways in which you might make connections.

Links

For more information on what to look for in poetry, see Chapter 4, pages 20–29.

The first pair to compare is a poem from 1789 by William Blake and a poem from 2010 by Michael Laskey.

Extract 1

'Nurse's Song' (C. 1789), William Blake

When voices of children are heard on the green
And laughing is heard on the hill,
My heart is at rest within my breast
And everything else is still

'Then come home my children: the sun is gone down
And the dews of night arise.
Come, come leave off play, and let us away,
Till the morning appears in the skies'

'No, no let us play, for it is yet day
And we cannot go to sleep.
Besides, in the sky the little birds fly,
And the hills are all covered with sheep.'

'Well, well go & play till the light fades away,
And then go home to bed.'
The little ones leaped & shouted & laugh'd
And all the hills echoed.

p17, *Songs of Innocence and of Experience* (Oxford University Press, 1990)

Extract 2

'Rain' (2010), Michael Laskey

So much rain, such a cloudburst, and the downpour
going on so long that the children
won't be fobbed off, they clamour
for their boots and cagoules, they jiggle
about while we unruck socks, struggle
with zips, but they're out in it now, arms flung wide,
rain tabooing their palms and their tongues,
wading in the lake on the gravel,
while we're back in the pantry mopping up,
bringing buckets and meat tins and cloths
to catch grey drips that keep tracking
through the tiles when the wind's in the east
that I said I'd get someone to fix
I'm reminded by that tightness in your lips,
so I settle to the job, shift stuff

off the shelves, clear the floor, the veg rack,
dry pears, wipe the spatter off onions.
Then later when I'm calling them in
for lunch, I find them squatting in the drive,
our heavy spades flat out beside
a land they've drained with canals
that connect and are linked to a sea
with its shingle beach where space
Lego figures stand waiting for a boat
to ground. Turning at my voice, they frown,
puzzled, as if they'd left me ages
before and can't make sense
of my English, my obsolete accent.

The Man Alone: New and Selected Poems

(Smith/Doorstop Books, 2010)

Activity 1

Comparing poems with similar subject matter

1. Start by reading these two poems a few times to familiarise yourself with the subject matter and how each poem might sound to your ear. What do you notice?

AO1

2. Identify the subject matter in more detail. Write a list of what you think each poem is about, any story being told or event being recalled, any description of people or places.

3. Identify the themes and concerns in each poem – what each poet wants to say about the event.

AOs 1 and 2

4. How is the subject matter presented in each poem? Remind yourself of poetic techniques you can compare from Chapter 4, pages 21–23.

AOs 1, 2 and 3

5. Compare the similarities and differences in subject matter and use of technique.

6. Compare how the mood and tone are created. What are the effects in each poem?

7. Who is the speaker and what is their role in each poem? Compare their viewpoints.

8. Compare the forms and structures. How do they help to present the subject matter and viewpoint of the poems?

AO3 (interpretations) and AO4 (reception)

9. Compare the effects of the poems on you. Where do your sympathies lie? Which poem do you prefer? Why?

10. Consider any differences you have found in the poems. Remind yourself of when they were written. What do you know about the contexts of each poem and how they might have influenced the writing? How does any contextual knowledge increase your understanding of the poems?

AOs 1, 2, 3 and 4

11. Compare the Blake poem with Extract 3 from Chapter 4 and answer questions 1–10 above.

12. If you are studying Blake, compare another poem from *Songs of Innocence and of Experience* with 'Rain'. If you are studying post-1990 poetry, compare any poem that makes connections with the Blake poem.

Commentary on Activity 1

Subject matter

In Activity 1, you compared two poems with a principal link: children playing outdoors and responses from children and their guardians to the end of playtime. Similar themes and ideas include the role of nature and experiences of the weather, the passage of time, domestic life and family relationships.

Technique

The use of voice is important in these poems. Both speakers guide your sympathies. The voice carries the attitudes to the children and their activity. The language of both of the speakers indicates their different view of the children at play and the relationships they each share with them.

The contrast in verse forms is important. Blake chooses a lyric form: quatrains with an ABCB rhyme scheme. It has a simple and regular structure and each line contains one complete idea or description. The form evokes the nursery rhyme, to reflect the innocence of the children and the caring tone of the Nurse.

Laskey uses free verse, and the lines bustle with energetic verbs like 'jiggle' and 'struggle', to show the energy and eagerness of the children. The use of enjambment carries actions from one line to the next as if the activities and experiences are ongoing, perhaps for too long in the speaker's view.

Context

Your comparative analysis might consider the similarities and differences in social and personal attitudes to play and the different presentations of the worlds in which the children are playing. For example, Blake's is based in untamed nature and Laskey's has a domestic feel. If you know anything about the contexts – for example, Blake's social, political and literary contexts – you will have some grasp of how and why they might be different. If you do not, you can still make several connections between the poems, as suggested under the sections 'Subject matter' and 'Technique'.

Now compare 'Mametz Wood' (2005) by Owen Sheers with 'Charge of the Light Brigade' (1854) by Alfred, Lord Tennyson, written 150 years earlier. These two poems present war and depict a specific military battle in British history. The first is a modern, retrospective reflection on soldiers who died in the Battle of the Somme (1916) during the First World War. It is written by a civilian from a distance of 90 years after the event, when there is still debate about who won that battle. The second is a contemporary Victorian reflection on soldiers who died in the Crimean War. It is written by the Poet Laureate of the time and was published in *The Examiner* only six weeks after the event. There is no question that this was a military loss of disastrous proportions. Consider how these two events are recalled, presented and explored.

Extract 3

'Mametz Wood' (2005), Owen Sheers

For years afterwards the farmers found them – the
wasted young, turning up under their plough blades
as they tended the land back into itself.

A chit of bone, the china plate of a shoulder blade,
the relic of a finger, the blown
and broken bird's egg of a skull,

all mimicked now in flint, breaking blue in white
across this field where they were told to walk, not run,
towards the wood and its nesting machine guns.

And even now the earth stands sentinel,
reaching back into itself for reminders of what happened
like a wound working on a foreign body to the surface
of the skin.

This morning, twenty men buried in one long grave,
a broken mosaic of bone linked arm in arm,
their skeletons paused mid dance-macabre

in boots that outlasted them,
their socketed heads tilted back at an angle
and their jaws, those that have them, dropped open.

As if the notes they had sung
have only now, with this unearthing,
slipped from their absent tongues.

p1, *Skirrid Hill* (Seren, 2005 edn)

Extract 4

'The Charge of the Light Brigade' (1854), Alfred, Lord Tennyson

1.

Half a league, half a league,
   Half a league onward,
All in the valley of Death
   Rode the six hundred.
'Forward, the Light Brigade!
'Charge for the guns!' he said:
Into the valley of Death
   Rode the six hundred.

2.

'Forward, the Light Brigade!'
Was there a man dismay'd?
Not tho' the soldier knew
   Someone had blunder'd:
Theirs not to make reply,
Theirs not to reason why,
Theirs but to do and die:
Into the valley of Death
   Rode the six hundred.

3.

Cannon to right of them,
Cannon to left of them,
Cannon in front of them
   Volley'd and thunder'd;
Storm'd at with shot and shell,
Boldly they rode and well,
Into the jaws of Death,
Into the mouth of Hell
   Rode the six hundred.

4.

Flash'd all their sabres bare,
Flash'd as they turn'd in air,
Sabring the gunners there,
Charging an army, while
   All the world wonder'd:
Plunged in the battery-smoke
Right thro' the line they broke;
Cossack and Russian
Reel'd from the sabre stroke
   Shatter'd and sunder'd.
Then they rode back, but not
   Not the six hundred.

5.

Cannon to right of them,
Cannon to left of them,
Cannon behind them
   Volley'd and thunder'd;
Storm'd at with shot and shell,
While horse and hero fell,
They that had fought so well
Came thro' the jaws of Death
Back from the mouth of Hell,
All that was left of them,
   Left of six hundred.

6.

When can their glory fade?
O the wild charge they made!
   All the world wondered.
Honor the charge they made,
Honor the Light Brigade,
   Noble six hundred.

Poems of Alfred Tennyson (J.E. Tilton and Company, 1870)

Activity 2

Comparing poems with different viewpoints
Start by reading these two poems a few times and considering the ways in which war and/or battle are presented.

AO1

1. Identify the subject matter more closely. What is being narrated and who is being described in these poems?

2. What different ideas and attitudes to war are expressed in each poem?

AO2

3. Examine the techniques each poem uses to present those differences.

AO2 and AO3

4. Compare the imagery of each poem and how it is used to describe the soldiers.

5. Examine the mood and tone of each poem. Compare how this is created.

AO3 (interpretations) and AO4 (reception)

6. Compare the effects of the subject matter and techniques on the reader.

7. Which poem do you prefer? Why?

8. How important do you find the different contexts of period: historically, politically, culturally and socially? For example, how do they illuminate the poems for you? How do you read the poems without them? What do the poems say to you in your own contexts?

9. Is this activity easier than Activity 1 because you are aware of some of the context? Why?

10. Do you think these poems are more similar than different? Why?

11. If you are studying war poetry, compare one or both of these poems with **either** Extract 1 **or** 2 in Chapter 4. Refer to questions 1–10 above.

Commentary on Activity 2

Subject matter

The poems present different aspects of war and battle. One poem is about dead soldiers after the battle and the other is about living soldiers going to die in battle.

Technique

The verbs convey different types of action and being. In both poems, the subject of the verbs is not always the British soldiers. This affects the presentation of the British soldiers and puts them on the receiving end of someone else's action. Sheers presents them as delicate victims and Tennyson presents them as brave and unstoppable.

The language use is very different. Tennyson's use of repetition, commands and rhetorical questioning is persuasive. This influences the mood of the poem and its effect on the reader. He wants you to see the soldiers as fighting men with a great cause. Sheers uses commas and dashes to create reflective and sombre pauses in your response to the wasted lives of the soldiers. His use of enjambment helps to convey the slow uncovering of wistful and poignant feelings expressed in the poem.

Context

There is an obvious shared overarching theme of war and men in battle. However, in these poems it is more than a theme. The subject matter of war in these two poems relates to specific, famous historical battles that are an important part of British social and cultural attitudes. The Tennyson poem reflects attitudes to our place in the world as a nation and empire. The Sheers poem reflects our contemporary response to the human cost of the First World War. This contextual knowledge creates strong connections between the poems even if they are different in their presentations of subject matter.

Prose

Below, you can compare two prose extracts: one is from the mid-19th century, during the Victorian era, and one is from the late 20th century. Consider how this affects the ways in which you might make connections.

Extract 5 is a novel extract from 1847 by Emily Brontë and Extract 6 is a short story extract from 1979, written 130 years later, by Angela Carter. These extracts are the opening of each text.

Link

For more information on what to look for in prose, see Chapter 4, pages 29–35.

Extract 5

Wuthering Heights (1847), Emily Brontë

1801. – I have just returned from a visit to my landlord – the solitary neighbour that I shall be troubled with.

This is certainly a beautiful country! In all England, I do not believe that I could have fixed on a situation so completely removed from the stir of society. A perfect misanthropist's Heaven: and Mr. Heathcliff and I are such a suitable pair to divide the desolation between us. A capital fellow! He little imagined how my heart warmed towards him when I beheld his black eyes withdraw so suspiciously under their brows, as I rode up, and when his fingers sheltered themselves, with a jealous resolution, still further in his waistcoat, as I announced my name.

'Mr. Heathcliff?' I said.

A nod was the answer.

'Mr. Lockwood, your new tenant, sir. I do myself the honour of calling as soon as possible after my arrival, to express the hope that I have not inconvenienced you by my perseverance in soliciting the occupation of Thrushcross Grange: I heard yesterday you had had some thoughts –'

'Thrushcross Grange is my own, sir,' he interrupted, wincing. 'I should not allow any one to inconvenience me, if I could hinder it – walk in!'

The 'walk in' was uttered with closed teeth, and expressed the sentiment, 'Go to the Deuce': even the gate over which he leant manifested no sympathising movement to the words; and I think that circumstance determined me to accept the invitation: I felt interested in a man who seemed more exaggeratedly reserved than myself.

When he saw my horse's breast fairly pushing the barrier, he did put out his hand to unchain it, and then sullenly preceded me up the causeway, calling, as we entered the court, – 'Joseph, take Mr. Lockwood's horse; and bring up some wine.'

'Here we have the whole establishment of domestics, I suppose,' was the reflection suggested by this compound order. 'No wonder the grass grows up between the flags, and cattle are the only hedge-cutters.'

Joseph was an elderly, nay, an old man: very old, perhaps, though hale and sinewy. 'The Lord help us!' he soliloquised in an undertone of peevish displeasure, while relieving me of my horse: looking, meantime, in my face so sourly that I charitably conjectured he must have need of divine aid to digest his dinner, and his pious ejaculation had no reference to my unexpected advent.

Wuthering Heights is the name of Mr. Heathcliff's dwelling. 'Wuthering' being a significant provincial adjective, descriptive of the atmospheric tumult to which its station is exposed in stormy weather. Pure, bracing ventilation they must have up there at all times, indeed: one may guess the power of the north wind blowing over the edge, by the excessive slant of a few stunted firs at the end of the house; and by a range of gaunt thorns all stretching their limbs one way, as if craving alms of the sun. Happily, the architect had foresight to build it strong: the narrow windows are deeply set in the wall, and the corners defended with large jutting stones.

Before passing the threshold, I paused to admire a quantity of grotesque carving lavished over the front, and especially about the principal door; above which, among a wilderness of crumbling griffins and shameless little boys, I detected the date '1500,' and the name 'Hareton Earnshaw.' I would have made a few comments, and requested a short history of the place from the surly owner; but his attitude at the door appeared to demand my speedy entrance, or complete departure, and I had no desire to aggravate his impatience previous to inspecting the penetralium.

One stop brought us into the family sitting-room, without any introductory lobby or passage: they call it here 'the house' pre-eminently. It includes kitchen and parlour, generally; but I believe at Wuthering Heights the kitchen is forced to retreat altogether into another quarter: at least I distinguished a chatter of tongues, and a clatter of culinary utensils, deep within; and I observed no signs of roasting, boiling, or baking, about the huge fireplace; nor any glitter of copper saucepans and tin cullenders on the walls. One end, indeed, reflected splendidly both light and heat from ranks of immense pewter dishes, interspersed with silver jugs and tankards, towering row after row, on a vast oak dresser, to the very roof. The latter had never been underdrawn: its entire anatomy lay bare to an inquiring eye, except where a frame of wood laden with oatcakes and clusters of legs of beef, mutton, and ham, concealed it. Above the chimney were sundry villainous old guns, and a couple of horse-pistols: and, by way of ornament, three gaudily-painted canisters disposed along its ledge. The floor was of smooth, white stone; the chairs, high-backed,

primitive structures, painted green: one or two heavy black ones lurking in the shade. In an arch under the dresser reposed a huge, liver-coloured bitch pointer, surrounded by a swarm of squealing puppies; and other dogs haunted other recesses.

The apartment and furniture would have been nothing extraordinary as belonging to a homely, northern farmer, with a stubborn countenance, and stalwart limbs set out to advantage in knee-breeches and gaiters.

Such an individual seated in his arm-chair, his mug of ale frothing on the round table before him, is to be seen in any circuit of five or six miles among these hills, if you go at the right time after dinner. But Mr. Heathcliff forms a singular contrast to his abode and style of living. He is a dark-skinned gipsy in aspect, in dress and manners a gentleman: that is, as much a gentleman as many a country squire: rather slovenly, perhaps, yet not looking amiss with his negligence, because he has an erect and handsome figure; and rather morose. Possibly, some people might suspect him of a degree of under-bred pride; I have a sympathetic chord within that tells me it is nothing of the sort: I know, by instinct, his reserve springs from an aversion to showy displays of feeling – to manifestations of mutual kindliness. He'll love and hate equally under cover, and esteem it a species of impertinence to be loved or hated again. No, I'm running on too fast: I bestow my own attributes over-liberally on him. Mr. Heathcliff may have entirely dissimilar reasons for keeping his hand out of the way when he meets a would-be acquaintance, to those which actuate me.

pp1–3, *Wuthering Heights* (Wordsworth Classics, 2000 edn [1847])

Extract 6
'The Bloody Chamber' (1979), Angela Carter

I remember how, that night, I lay awake in the wagon-lit in a tender, delicious ecstasy of excitement, my burning cheek pressed against the impeccable linen of the pillow and the pounding of my heart mimicking that of the great pistons ceaselessly thrusting the train that bore me through the night, away from Paris, away from girlhood, away from the white, enclosed quietude of my mother's apartment, into the unguessable country of marriage.

And I remember I tenderly imagined how, at this very moment, my mother would be moving slowly about the narrow bedroom I had left behind for ever, folding up and putting away all my little relics, the tumbled garments I would not need any more, the scores for which there had been no room in my trunks, the concert programmes I'd abandoned; she would linger

over this torn ribbon and that faded photograph with all the half-joyous, half-sorrowful emotions of a woman on her daughter's wedding day. And, in the midst of my bridal triumph, I felt a pang of loss as if, when he put the gold band on my finger, I had, in some way, ceased to be her child in becoming his wife.

Are you sure, she'd said when they delivered the gigantic box that held the wedding dress he'd bought me, wrapped up in tissue paper and red ribbon like a Christmas gift of crystallized fruit. Are you sure you love him? There was a dress for her, too; black silk, with the dull, prismatic sheen of oil on water, finer than anything she'd worn since that adventurous girlhood in Indo-China, daughter of a rich tea planter. My eagle-featured, indomitable mother; what other student at the Conservatoire could boast that her mother had outfaced a junkful of Chinese pirates, nursed a village through a visitation of the plague, shot a man-eating tiger with her own hand and all before she was as old as I?

'Are you sure you love him?'

'I'm sure I want to marry him,' I said.

And would say no more. She sighed, as if it was with reluctance that she might at last banish the spectre of poverty from its habitual place at our meagre table. For my mother herself had gladly, scandalously, defiantly beggared herself for love; and, one fine day, her gallant soldier never returned from the wars, leaving his wife and child a legacy of tears that never quite dried, a cigar box full of medals and the antique service revolver that my mother, grown magnificently eccentric in hardship, kept always in her reticule, in case – how I teased her – she was surprised by footpads on her way home from the grocer's shop.

Now and then a starburst of lights spattered the drawn blinds as if the railway company had lit up all the stations through which we passed in celebration of the bride. My satin nightdress had just been shaken from its wrappings; it had slipped over my young girl's pointed breasts and shoulders, supple as a garment of heavy water, and now teasingly caressed me, egregious, insinuating, nudging between my thighs as I shifted restlessly in my narrow berth. His kiss, his kiss with tongue and teeth in it and a rasp of beard, had hinted to me, though with the same exquisite tact as this nightdress he'd given me, of the wedding night, which would be voluptuously deferred until we lay in his great ancestral bed in the sea-girt, pinnacled domain that lay, still, beyond the grasp of my imagination ... that magic place, the fairy castle whose walls were made of foam, that legendary habitation in which he had been born. To which, one day, I might bear an heir. Our destination, my destiny.

Above the syncopated roar of the train, I could hear his even, steady breathing. Only the communicating door kept me from my husband and it stood open. If I rose up on my elbow, I could see the dark, leonine shape of his head and my nostrils caught a whiff of the opulent male scent of leather and spices that always accompanied him and sometimes, during his courtship, had been the only hint he gave me that he had come into my mother's sitting room, for, though he was a big man, he moved as softly as if all his shoes had soles of velvet, as if his footfall turned the carpet into snow.

He had loved to surprise me in my abstracted solitude at the piano. He would tell them not to announce him, then soundlessly open the door and softly creep up behind me with his bouquet of hot-house flowers or his box of marrons glacés, lay his offering upon the keys and clasp his hands over my eyes as I was lost in a Debussy prelude. But that perfume of spiced leather always betrayed him; after my first shock, I was forced always to mimic surprise, so that he would not be disappointed.

He was older than I. He was much older than I; there were streaks of pure silver in his dark mane. But his strange, heavy, almost waxen face was not lined by experience. Rather, experience seemed to have washed it perfectly smooth, like a stone on a beach whose fissures have been eroded by successive tides. And sometimes that face, in stillness when he listened to me playing, with the heavy eyelids folded over eyes that always disturbed me by their absolute absence of light, seemed to me like a mask, as if his real face, the face that truly reflected all the life he had led in the world before he met me, before, even, I was born, as though that face lay underneath this mask. Or else, elsewhere. As though he had laid by the face in which he had lived for so long in order to offer my youth a face unsigned by the years.

And, elsewhere, I might see him plain. Elsewhere. But, where?

In, perhaps, that castle to which the train now took us, that marvellous castle in which he had been born.

pp1–3, *The Bloody Chamber and Other Stories* (Penguin, 1979)

Activity 3

Comparing prose openings

1. Start by reading these extracts a few times and jotting down what you notice. Remember that they are the opening paragraphs of each text.

AO1

2. Identify the subject matter: the introduction to each of the plots, characters and settings.

AOs 1 and 3

3. What connections can you make about the subject matter at this stage?

AO2

4. Examine how the stories are told or introduced.

AOs 2 and 3

5. Examine the presentation of each narrator. Compare their roles in the events of the texts so far. Compare their effect on your response to the introduction to each text.

6. Compare the presentations of time, reflection and recall. How do you imagine what happens next?

7. Compare the presentation of characters.

8. Compare the importance of the settings. How are they symbolic?

9. How do the settings present the mood and tone of the extracts?

AO4

10. What do you know about the contexts of these extracts?

11. Compare the influence of the material world of either 1847 or 1979, outside of the texts. (It is complicated by the fact that both texts are set earlier than their composition date. Some critics say that this does not matter: the texts tell you something about how writers in 1847 and 1979 see the worlds they present in the texts, influenced by the ones they come from themselves.)

AOs 2 and 4

12. If you are studying any (other) Victorian texts, compare ways in which Extract 5 shares some narrative techniques with mid-19th-century novel openings.

Commentary on Activity 3

Subject matter

Both extracts feature a character going to live in strange surroundings, far away from their familiar societies and domestic habits. One is a young bride on a journey of sensual discovery, and the other is an older man looking to settle down. The descriptions of people and places show how they are both utterly out of their depth.

Technique

Both of these narrators are compelling because their viewpoints and relationships, presented as naive, draw you into the plot and what might happen next. As a result, each extract shares a mood of strong foreboding built into the introductions. The use of symbols echoes the threat of danger and violence in the mood and tone of each extract. For example, the presentation of animals, smells, clothes, food, and so on, are used as metaphors for the sexuality of the bride and her husband, the masculinity of Heathcliff and the lack of manliness and sexuality of Lockwood.

Both descriptions of people, places and feelings contribute to the unsettling mood. We are introduced to characters that we would not trust, even though the narrators might do: Heathcliff, who has only one name, and the narrator's husband, only referred to as 'he'. Even though 'he' is named elsewhere in Carter's text, this is a long extract from a short story, so the sustained absence of his name here is important. His status is that of a man of mystery about whom the narrator knows little. Brontë gives 'Heathcliff' this name, which combines the two places where he lives: on high moors. This suggests that he is far from the quiet domestic farmer and is wild and dangerous, like the elements in his name.

Context

The literary contexts of these two texts are very helpful in making connections. For example, both are seen as containing elements of Gothic literature and use many of the conventions of this subgenre. If you are studying the Gothic, compare how these introductions conform to or reject the label of 'Gothic'. If you are studying texts which feature fantasy, fairy-tale elements, the supernatural and/or the magic realist subgenre, compare how far these introductions demonstrate the conventions of those styles.

Some critics argue that *Wuthering Heights* stands apart from typical Victorian novels because it seems to transcend time and ignore the social conditions beyond the local settings (compared with, say, Charles Dickens). Other critics disagree and think it sets the social, political and cultural scene very clearly (compared with, say, Thomas Hardy), through the choices, settings and outcomes of the characters.

Drama

In this section, you can compare two drama extracts from the late 16th century and the late 20th century, 400 years apart. The two drama extracts in Chapter 4 were tragedies. Here, one is a romantic comedy and the other has many comic elements, although it is not entirely a comedy. See how this affects the ways in which you might make connections.

This extract comes from Act 3, Scene 3, the mid-point of a five-act play. Rosalind, the romantic heroine, is in love with Orlando, a lord. He has written her a love poem and pinned it to a tree in the forest where they have already met but are each hiding and travelling separately with their companions. Rosalind is disguised a young man, to protect her from danger in the forest and free her from the social roles she occupies outside it. Here, Rosalind finds the poem and discusses it with Touchstone, her fool, a sort of advisory servant.

> **Link**
>
> For more information in what to look for in drama, see Chapter 4 pages 35–40.

> ## Extract 7
> *As You Like It* (c.1599), **William Shakespeare**
> *Enter Rosalind* [*as Ganymede*]
> ROSALIND [*Reading from a paper*]
> 'From the East to Western Inde
> No jewel is like Rosalind;
> Her worth, being mounted on the wind,
> Through all the world bears Rosalind;
> All the pictures fairest lined

Are but black to Rosalind;
Let no face be kept in mind
But the fair of Rosalind.'
TOUCHSTONE
I'll rhyme you so eight years together, dinners and suppers and sleeping-
hours excepted. It is the right butter-women's rank to market.
ROSALIND
Out, fool!
TOUCHSTONE
For a taste:
If a hart do lack a hind,
Let him seek out Rosalind;
If the cat will after kind,
So be sure will Rosalind;
Wintered garments must be lined,
So must slender Rosalind;
They that reap must sheaf and blind,
Then to cart with Rosalind;
Sweetest nut hath sourest rind,
Such a nut is Rosalind;
He that sweetest rose will find,
Must find love's prick – and Rosalind.
This is the very false gallop of verse: why do you infect yourself
with them?
ROSALIND
Peace, you dull fool. I found them on a tree.
TOUCHSTONE
Truly, the tree yields bad fruit.
ROSALIND
I'll graft it with you, and then I shall graft it with a medlar; then it will be
the earliest fruit i'th'country, for you'll be rotten ere you be half active,
and that's the right virtue of the medlar.
TOUCHSTONE
You have said – but whether wisely or no, let the forest judge.

Act 3, Scene 3, lines 65–98, pp 148–150, New Cambridge
Shakespeare 2000, 2009 edn (Cambridge University Press, 2000)

Arcadia has a complex dramatic structure that spans two time periods, 1809
and 1993, when the play was written. The action takes place in one setting,
a large country estate called Sidley Park. This scene is set in the earlier
time and features Lady Croom, the mistress of the house, and Septimus
Hodge, her daughter's tutor. They are sexually attracted to each other. This
exchange is over a letter Hodge has sent her, declaring his feelings, only for
her to find he has just had sex with someone else's wife, Mrs Chater, who is a
guest at the house.

Extract 8

Arcadia (1993), Tom Stoppard
LADY CROOM
Your letter to me goes very ill with your conduct to Mrs Chater, Mr
Hodge. I have had experiences of being betrayed before the ink is dry,
but to be betrayed before the pen is even dipped, and with the village
noticeboard, what am I to think of such a performance?

SEPTIMUS

My lady, I was alone with my thoughts in the gazebo, when Mrs Chater ran me to ground, and I being in such a passion, in an agony of unrelieved desire –

LADY CROOM

Oh…!

SEPTIMUS

– I thought in my madness that the Chater with her skirts over her head would give me the momentary illusion of the happiness to which I dared not put a face.

Pause.

LADY CROOM

I do not know when I have received a more unusual compliment, Mr Hodge. I hope I am more than a match for Mrs Chater with her head in a bucket. Does she wear drawers?

SEPTIMUS

She does.

LADY CROOM

Yes, I have heard that drawers are being worn now. It is unnatural for women to be got up like jockeys. I cannot approve. [*She turns with a whirl of skirts and moves to leave.*] I know nothing of Pericles or the Athenian philosophers. I can spare them an hour, in my sitting room when I have bathed. Seven o'clock. Bring a book.

She goes out. Septimus picks up the two letters, the ones he wrote, and starts to burn them in the flame of the spirit lamp.

Act 2, Scene 6, pp97–9, *Arcadia* (Faber and Faber, 1999 edn)

Activity 4

Comparing dramatic language and form

1. Read these extracts a few times and note what you think they are about.

AO1

2. Identify the messages about romantic love and sexual attraction.

AOs 1 and 2

3. How are relationships between characters presented?

AOs 1, 2 and 3

4. Examine ways in which love and desire are declared. How are the extracts similar and different in professing romantic and sexual feelings?

5. Compare how the mood is created in each text.

AOs 1, 2, 3 and 4

6. Examine and compare the comic elements of the extracts.

7. These two plays are sometimes studied together as Elements of the Pastoral. If you study pastoral elements in your texts, examine how the natural world is presented in these two scenes and/or how social structures, such as social class, are operating within the relationships and the expectations of the audience of the time.

8. Mistaken identity and disguise are important in both of these plays, and this is a typical element of romantic comedy. How do Shakespeare and Stoppard use 'pretending to be someone else or in an altered state' in these two extracts?

9. Why do you think that Stoppard uses language that is not typical of any English society in 1993, when it was written?

Commentary on Activity 4

Subject matter

Both extracts feature a character professing romantic love or desire for another. The episodes show that they are both welcomed. Shakespeare and Stoppard both mock ideas about romantic love and lovesick lovers.

Technique

The level of formality between the characters and the way they address each other is an interesting comparison. Stoppard uses a comic-formal tone and vocabulary to present Lady Croom's status and to mock romantic encounters. Shakespeare uses the clown to present the lovers as ridiculous and to mock their flirtation.

The dialogue in both extracts uses language associated with sex and love. The conventions of love letters and love poems are used both as forms to profess love and as ways for the writers to create comedy from the actions of the senders and receivers.

Contexts

Both extracts use the comic convention of absent lovers. Shakespeare uses this feature to create a plot that hinges on disguise and deception, also typical conventions of romantic comedy. Stoppard uses Mrs Chater, a minor character, to present the shallowness of romantic encounters such as hers with Hodge.

Reflecting on cross-period comparisons

You have now compared extracts from each genre across the past five centuries.

These extracts and activities offer starting points on how to approach detailed comparative analysis, and to read closely so that the bigger links you make will be grounded in evidence. They should show you that despite time and period differences, texts that initially appear far apart can often be meaningfully connected. This should enable you to understand them better as individual works and as examples of their genre, period and/or literary tradition.

If you study the whole texts for comparison – novels, plays and poetry collections – and you study them in context, you will inevitably make richer connections between the texts than you have been able to make in this chapter.

> **Think about it**
>
> **Comparing extracts in context**
> Which pair of extracts from Chapter 5 do you think most relies on a grasp of their social and literary contexts. How and why?

> **Summary**
>
> This chapter has introduced you to comparing texts from the same genre, but across different periods. You should now be able to identify similarities and differences and do a comparative analysis of a range of cross-period examples of:
>
> - poetry
> - prose
> - drama.

6 Same period, different genre

Chapter aims

In this chapter we will look at how to compare texts from the same period but from different genres. We will consider finding similarities and differences between:

- poetry and prose
- prose and drama
- drama and poetry
- all three genres.

Remember

Defining period and era

How long is a period or era? In literature, a period is an identifiable time-span with a commonly accepted beginning and end; it is determined by generally recognisable and important key events, dates and/or major historical figures (often monarchs). Period is not determined by length of time. For example, the literary period of post-1990 texts is currently 23 years, the First World War period is about 10 years, and the Elizabethan and Jacobean period is about 50 years.

Links

For more information on techniques in each genre, see Chapter 4, pages 20–29 for poetry, pages 29–35 for prose, and pages 35–40 for drama.

Finding similarities and differences

Comparing texts from the same period and different genres can be more challenging than the comparisons you have made in Chapters 4 and 5. Comparing texts from the same period means that your texts could share similar ways in which they reflect the concerns of the time. Texts from different genres are more likely to use different techniques. Poetic, narrative or dramatic language, structure and form can vary greatly as part of their genre conventions. As a result, a cross-genre comparison, where you address AO2, can often be more challenging and requires a slightly different approach.

Contexts

Period

Identify the similarities that a shared period creates in your texts. Look at how the society, or societies, of the time turn to literature to express its concerns. For example, consider how context shapes the literary concerns of the Elizabethan and Jacobean period, the Romantic period, the Victorian period and the period of the First World War. The Jacobeans reflected on how violence, death and the supernatural were viewed in their society. Romantic writers explored social concerns about how children were viewed and treated at the time. The Victorians demonstrated their concerns about how industrialisation and poverty had affected society. The First World War writers reflected on the ways in which this war had changed their society.

Look at any divisions within the period to uncover differences in your texts, such as significant cultural and historical events or turning points. For example, examine any differences between texts from 1914, when the war began, and from 1918, when it was ending; texts from the early and late Victorian period; texts from the first generation of the Romantics, such as Blake, and the second generation, such as Keats; and texts by the Elizabethan Marlowe and the Jacobean Webster.

You might also notice how one particular genre seems to be more popular in certain eras. If you are comparing across genres within the period, look at how and why the period might have caused one genre to be more well-known than another. You are likely to find that each era contains a 'golden age', or flowering and development, of a particular genre or one or more of its subgenres – for example, the 19th-century novel. By the mid 20th century, literary movements are equally reflected across the genres of poetry, prose and drama written in English. One example is European and North American Modernism in the 1920s and 1930s.

Subject matter

Themes

Identify any shared themes and concerns in your texts. Consider whether the texts explore any shared universal themes. Examine if the themes are particularly relevant to the period, such as the examples at the start of the section above on 'Period'. Consider which interests your writers share. It might be that their messages connect your same-period texts.

Technique

Use of voice

Compare the uses of characterisation, speakers and viewpoints. For example, look at whether your texts are interested in the fortunes of kings or the common man, the ordinary soldier and worker or rich and privileged individuals and social groups. Examine how the writers show you what interests them about how people behaved, thought and felt at the time. Examine the mode/s of address and the relationship/s of characters, narrators and speakers with the reader or audience.

Choice of genre

The different choice of genre that your writers make affects connections between texts from the same period. You might have begun by uncovering similarities in the subject matter, concerns and voices of the period. You might then find that significant differences occur through the choice of genre in the ways that the subject matter is presented. For example, post-1990 drama and poetry might deal with similar issues of social injustice in different ways because of their genres.

In the play *Murmuring Judges* (1991), David Hare makes harsh criticisms of the failure of justice and corruption of the judicial system in a range of London settings. He is concerned with attitudes to minorities and immigrants and uses a split-narrative structure and a series of interior monologues. Hare does this to present the cases of his central characters that are socially isolated and caught up in injustice like flies in a web. The play is a tragedy, with some of the conventions of that subgenre. By contrast, the poem 'Translating the English' (1990) by Carol Ann Duffy has the same concerns of attitudes to minorities and immigrants, but uses parody. She presents the speaker as an immigrant who tries to make England seem a welcoming place, while warning you of the pitfalls of coming here in a tone of false jollity. Hare's split narrative structure works through separate set scenes involving appropriately chosen characters – professional and lay people – who express differing points of view through dialogue. Duffy's parody involves a single voice, brought to life through apt choices of vocabulary, language patterns and cultural references.

Forms and subgenres

Despite the genre differences, you might find that there are several similarities in the ways in which the subject matter is presented. Different genres use different forms, but there could be common subgenres connecting your texts, such as science fiction or magic realism, which became popular in the 1980s, but is in evidence in texts from the 1950s onwards. You can examine an example of how subgenre can link texts of the same period and a different genre later in the chapter, in Activity 3. The link is influenced by the ways in which the literary contexts of a particular period connect texts with different genres but shared concerns.

Language

Examine how word choices in your texts can present a particular verse, episode or scene. Explore how those words tell you what concerns and connects the writers at those points in the texts. Look at how language creates the mood or tone in each text – for example, to make it tense or funny. Examine whether the mood typically demonstrates any concerns, subgenres or language use from the period.

Typicality

Evaluate how macro and literary contexts influence 'the literature of the period'. After examining how the use of subject matter and technique links your texts from the same period, step back and see how the contexts

> **Key terms**
>
> **Interior monologue** like a **stream of consciousness** but spoken (rather than just thought or written) by the character and directed at the audience.
>
> **Stream of consciousness** naturalistic language providing an uninterrupted 'stream' of the characters' thoughts and feelings.
>
> **Parody** an imitation of the style of a particular writer, artist, genre, subgenre voice or individual, with deliberate exaggeration for comic effect.
>
> **Magic realism** a movement which blends the styles of a fairy tale or mythical fantasy and harsh social reality. Both plays and novels use this style.
>
> **Macro** the overview or 'big picture': these contexts are concerned with the world outside of the text – historical and political, social and cultural.

influence the ways in which texts are 'typical' of their time. You might find that there are groups within groups in the same period, particularly if you are looking at several texts for **wider reading** or how **partner texts** support and emphasise key ideas and techniques within a **core text**. For example, if all your texts are post-1990, you might see that some share a typical post-1990 concern of representing the Second World War from German children's viewpoints, as evident in the novel *Spies* (2002) by Michael Frayn and the play *Kindertransport* (1995) by Diane Samuels. You might see how some share a typical modern subject matter of presenting soldiers as ordinary men in suffering who are afraid and vulnerable. Even more interesting is the typical contemporary concern that we feel guilt because we cannot comprehend or change the suffering of our ancestors and families: for example, the pathos or harrowing grief we witness and are directed to feel ourselves in the poem 'Mametz Wood' (2005) by Owen Sheers, and in the novels *Birdsong* (1993) by Sebastian Faulks and *The Ghost Road* (1995) by Pat Barker.

Let us consider some examples of cross-genre connections of texts from the same period.

Poetry and prose

Here we compare a poem and an extract from early on in the novel. Both were published within a year of each other, Extract 1 first appearing in 1983, and Extract 2 in 1982, and both have been influenced by the earlier political movements of civil rights and feminism that developed in the 1960s and 1970s. During the 1980s, many writers became especially interested in revisiting the domestic and sexual experiences and the status of black women and girls. These texts are examples of social and cultural responses to the position of black women in slavery, and then within their own families in segregated society in the aftermath of slavery. The forms are very different. The poem is in free verse with an irregular verse structure. The novel opening is a series of informal letters.

Grace Nichols is from Guyana in the Caribbean and has lived in London since the 1970s. Alice Walker is an African American and lives in the USA. Both writers are female.

Extract 1
'Loveact' (1983), Grace Nichols

She enters into his Great House
her see-far looking eyes
unassuming

He fix her with his glassy stare
and feel the thin fire in his blood
awakening

Soon she is the fuel
that keep them all going

He/his mistresswife/and his
children who take to her breasts
like leeches

He want to tower above her
want her to raise her ebony

haunches and when she does
he think she can be trusted
and drinks her in

and his mistresswife
spending her days in rings
of vacant smiling
is glad to be rid of the
loveact

But time pass/es

Her sorcery cut them
like a whip

She hide her triumph
And slowly stir the hate
of poison in

p54, *The Fat Black Woman's Poems* (Virago, 1984)

Extract 2

The Color Purple (1982), Alice Walker

Dear God,

He beat me today cause he say I winked at a boy in church. I may have got somethin in my eye but I didn't wink. I don't even look at mens. That's the truth. I look at women, tho, cause I'm not scared of them. Maybe cause my mama cuss me you think I kept mad at her. But I ain't. I felt sorry for mama. Trying to believe his story kilt her.

Sometime he still be looking at Nettie, but I always git in his light. Now I tell her to marry Mr —. I don't tell her why.

I say Marry him, Nettie, an try to have one good year out your life. After that, I know she be big.

But me, never again. A girl at church say you git big if you bleed every month. I don't bleed no more.

[…]

Dear God

Harpo ast his daddy why he beat me. Mr — say, Cause she my wife. Plus, she stubborn. All women good for – he don't finish. He just tuck his chin over the paper like he do. Remind me of Pa.

Harpo ast me, How come you stubborn? He don't ast How come you his wife? Nobody ast that.

I say, Just born that way, I reckon.

He beat me like he beat the children. Cept he don't never hardly beat them. He say, Celie, git the belt. The children be outside the room peeking through the cracks. It all I can do not to cry. I make myself wood. I say to myself, Celie, you are a tree. That's how I come to know trees fear man.

Harpo say, I love Somebody.

I say, Huh?

He say, A Girl.

I say, You do?

He say, Yeah. Us plan to marry.

Marry, I say. You're not old enough to marry.

I is, he say. I'm seventeen. She fifteen. Old enough.

What her mamma say, I ast.

Further reading

Compare the following with 'Loveact' on experiences of slavery:

- *Beloved* (1987), Toni Morrison – set in the 19th-century southern US.

Compare with *The Color Purple* on experiences of childhood:

- *The Bluest Eye* (1970), Toni Morrison – set in the segregated southern US
- 'Be a Butterfly' (1984), Grace Nichols – set in Caribbean Guyana.

Ain't talk to her mama.

What her daddy say?

Ain't talk to him neither.

Well, what *she* say?

Us ain't never spoke. He duck his head. He ain't so bad looking. Tall and skinny, black like his mama, with great big bug eyes.

Where yall see each other? I ast. I see her in church, he say. She see me outdoors.

She like you?

I don't know. I wink at her. She act like she scared to look.

Where her daddy at while this going on?

Amen corner, he say.

pp7 and 23–24, *The Color Purple* (Phoenix, 2004 edn [1982])

Activity 1

Comparing poetry and prose

Read Extracts 1 and 2 and answer the following questions.

AO1

1. What is happening in each extract?

2. Identify any themes.

AOs 1 and 3

3. How is their subject matter similar and different?

AOs 1, 2 and 3

4. How are the characters described in each extract?

5. Compare how they are presented.

AOs 1 and 2

6. Who is the speaker or narrator in each extract?

7. Examine how each writer uses accent, dialect and colloquialism to tell the story.

8. Examine the use of dialogue in each extract.

AOs 1, 2 and 3

9. Compare ways in which the narrators speak to the reader.

10. Compare the language use in the extracts and the way each writer tells the story.

AOs 2 and 4

11. What is the social status of the narrators in the setting within each extract? How do you know?

AOs 1, 2, 3 and 4

12. Both extracts are from the early 1980s. Identify and evaluate any shared contexts that help you to make connections between them.

13. If you are studying either of these texts to explore any same-period/different-genre comparisons, examine any connections you find between them and one of the suggested texts for Further reading on page 61.

Prose and drama

Here we compare an extract from the beginning of a novel from 1969 and the opening scene of a play from 1958. They were published in a period that was defined by the aftermath of the Second World War. These texts are examples of social and cultural responses to the horrors of that war.

Slaughterhouse 5 by Kurt Vonnegut is an example of the type of novel which features a hero or heroine who lacks a sense of belonging with the wider social or cultural contexts around them. The central character of this type of novel is an outsider, unable to cope with the practical and emotional realities of day-to-day life and the concept of human living. He or she rejects the values of the society around him or her and chooses to withdraw. This withdrawal from society can be presented as mental and/or literal. The motivation for withdrawal may range from a character's response to a trauma or a complete lack of identification with the material world and its beliefs and priorities. This is typical of the prose fiction emerging after the Second World War as part of the cultural and literary movement of **existentialism**.

Compare this extract with *Endgame* by Samuel Beckett. Most plays you study have a plot in which events that happen to the characters are the driving force of the drama. Beckett instead places characters in dramatic settings where nothing happens at all. The only 'reality' of their situation is a psychological reality and the humdrum nature of everyday life. Life, society and people are presented as dysfunctional. The limited action and lack of a functioning world are features of the Theatre of the Absurd – which was influenced by the same existentialist movement that influenced Vonnegut in his creation of the alternative reality in *Slaughterhouse 5*.

These cross-genre same-period texts are connected through some of the shared literary, social and cultural contexts of their time. Let us look at some of the ways in which a period can produce typical texts through shared subgenres and movements.

Extract 3 is from *Slaughterhouse 5* (1969) by Kurt Vonnegut. This extract is taken from near the beginning of the novel, when the hero, Billy, is first presented to the reader. Vonnegut uses this early episode to prepare the reader for the split narrative which follows throughout the novel.

> ### Extract 3
> *Slaughterhouse 5* (1969), Kurt Vonnegut
>
> LISTEN:
> BILLY PILGRIM has come unstuck in time.
> Billy has gone to sleep a senile widower and awakened on his wedding day. He has walked through a door in 1955 and come out another one in 1941. He has gone back through that door to find himself in 1963. He has seen his birth and death many times, he says, and pays random visits to all the events in between.
> HE SAYS,
> Billy is spastic in time, has no control over where he is going next, and the trips aren't necessarily fun. He is in a state of stage fright, he says, because he never knows what part of his life he is going to have to act in next.
> Billy was born in 1922 in Ilium, New York, the only child of a barber there.

Key term

Existentialism a philosophical theory based on the existence of the individual as a free and responsible agent determining his or her own development. A central idea is that God is dead and that life has no other meaning than what we give it.

Did you know?

Theatre of the Absurd
The Theatre of the Absurd shows human beings outside of a historical, social or cultural context. It does not communicate any general views of human life.

He was a funny-looking youth – tall and weak and shaped like a bottle of Coca-Cola. He graduated from Ilium High School in the upper third of his class, and attended night sessions at the Ilium School of Optometry for one semester before being drafted for military service in the Second World War. His father died in a hunting accident during the war. So it goes. Billy saw service with the infantry in Europe, and was taken prisoner by the Germans. After his honorable discharge from the Army in 1945, Billy again enrolled in the Ilium School of Optometry. During his senior year there, he became engaged to the daughter of the founder and owner of the school, and then suffered a mild nervous collapse.

He was treated in a veteran's hospital near Lake Placid, and was given shock treatments and released. He married his fiancée, finished his education, and was set up in business in Ilium by his father-in-law. Ilium is a particularly good city for optometrists because the General Gorge and Foundry Company is there. Every employee is required to own a pair of safety glasses, and to wear them in areas where manufacturing is going on. GF&F has sixty-eight thousand employees in Ilium. That calls for a lot of lenses and a lot of frames. Frames are where the money is.

Billy became rich. He had two children, Barbara and Robert. In time, his daughter Barbara married another optometrist, and Billy set him up in business. Billy's son Robert had a lot of trouble in high school, but then he joined the famous Green Berets. He straightened out, became a fine young man, and he fought in Vietnam.

Early in 1968, a group of optometrists, with Billy among them, chartered an airplane to fly them from Ilium to an international convention of optometrists in Montreal. The plane crashed on top of Sugarbush Mountain, in Vermont. Everybody was killed but Billy. So it goes.

While Billy was recuperating in a hospital in Vermont, his wife died accidentally of carbon-monoxide poisoning. So it goes.

When Billy finally got home to Ilium after the airplane crash, he was quiet for a while. He had a terrible scar across the top of his skull. He didn't resume practice. He had a housekeeper. His daughter came over almost every day. And then, without any warning, Billy went to New York City, and got on an all-night radio program devoted to talk. He told about having come unstuck in time. He said, too, that he had been kidnapped by a flying saucer in 1967. The saucer was from the planet Tralfamadore, he said. He was taken to Tralfamadore, where he was displayed naked in a zoo, he said. He was mated there with a former Earthling movie star named Montana Wildhack. Some night owls in Ilium heard Billy on the radio, and one of them called Billy's daughter Barbara. Barbara was upset. She and her husband went down to New York and brought Billy home. Billy insisted mildly that everything he had said on the radio was true. He said he had been kidnapped by the Tralfamadorians on the night of his daughter's wedding. He hadn't been missed, he said, because the Tralfamadorians had taken him through a time warp, so that he could be on Tralfamadore for years, and still be away from Earth for only a microsecond.

Another month went by without incident, and then Billy wrote a letter to the Ilium *News Leader*, which the paper published. It described the creatures from Tralfamadore.

The letter said that they were two feet high, and green, and shaped like plumber's friends. Their suction cups were on the ground, and their shafts, which were extremely flexible, usually pointed to the sky. At the top of each shaft was a little hand with a green eye in its palm. The creatures were friendly, and they could see in four dimensions. They pitied Earthlings for being able to see only three. They had many wonderful things to teach Earthlings, especially about time. Billy promised to tell what some of those wonderful things were in his next letter.

Billy was working on his second letter when the first letter was published. The second letter started out like this:

'The most important thing I learned on Tralfamadore was that when a person dies he only *appears* to die. He is still very much alive in the past, so it is very silly for people to cry at his funeral. All moments, past, present, and future, always have existed, always will exist. The Tralfamadorians can look at all the different moments just the way we can look at a stretch of the Rocky Mountains, for instance. They can see how permanent all the moments are, and they can look at any moment that interests them. It is just an illusion we have here on Earth that one moment follows another one, like beads on a string, and that once a moment is gone it is gone forever.

'When a Tralfamadorian sees a corpse, all he thinks is that the dead person is in bad condition in that particular moment, but that the same person is just fine in plenty of other moments. Now, when I myself hear that someone is dead, I simply shrug and say what the Tralfamadorians say about dead people, which is "So it goes."'

pp17–20, *Slaughterhouse 5* (Vintage, 2000 edn [1969])

The protagonists of *Endgame* are Hamm, an aged master, who is blind and cannot stand up, and his servant Clov, who cannot sit down. They exist in perpetual conflict in a tiny house by the sea. The dialogue suggests that there is no exterior left – no sea, no sun, no clouds – and the way in which the stage directions focus on windows helps to highlight this lack of an external world.

Extract 4

Endgame (1958), Samuel Beckett

Bare interior. Grey light. Left and right back, high up, two small windows, curtains drawn. Front right, a door. Hanging near door, its face to wall, a picture. Front left, touching each other, covered with an old sheet, two ashbins. Centre, in an armchair on castors, covered with an old sheet, HAMM. *Motionless by the door, his eyes fixed on* HAMM, CLOV. *Very red face. Brief tableau.*

CLOV goes and stands under window left. Stiff, staggering walk. He looks up at window left. He turns and looks at window right. He goes and stands under window right. He looks up at window right. He turns and looks at window left. He goes out, comes back immediately with a small step-ladder, carries it over and sets it down under window left, gets up on it, draws back curtain. He gets down, takes six steps [for example] towards window right, goes back for ladder, carries it over and sets it down under window right, gets up on it, draws back curtain. He gets down, takes three steps towards window left, goes back for ladder, carries it over and sets it down under

Think about it

Dramatic and narrative structure

Extracts 3 and 4 come from texts with contrasting structures.

Endgame is a one-act play. After your reading of the extract, consider why Beckett chose this dramatic structure for the play.

Slaughterhouse 5 has a split-narrative structure. Why do you think Vonnegut chose a structure that swaps between worlds, settings and realities in this novel?

window left, gets up on it, looks out of window. Brief laugh. He gets down, takes one step towards window right, goes back for ladder, carries it over and sets it down under window right, gets up on it, looks out of window. Brief laugh. He gets down, goes with ladder towards ashbins, halts, turns, carries back ladder and sets it down under window right, goes to ashbins, removes sheet covering them, folds it over his arm. He raises one lid, stoops and looks into bin. Brief laugh. He closes lid. Same with other bin. He goes to HAMM, removes sheet covering him, folds it over his arm. In a dressing-gown, a stiff toque on his head, a large blood-stained handkerchief over his face, a whistle hanging from his neck, a rug over his knees, thick socks on his feet, HAMM seems to be asleep. CLOV looks him over. Brief laugh. He goes to door, halts, turns towards auditorium.

CLOV

[*Fixed gaze, tonelessly.*] Finished, it's finished, nearly finished, it must be nearly finished. [*Pause.*] Grain upon grain, one by one, and one day, suddenly, there's a heap, a little heap, the impossible heap. [*Pause.*] I'll go now to my kitchen, ten feet by ten feet by ten feet, and wait for him to whistle me. [*Pause.*] Nice dimensions, nice proportions, I'll lean on the table, and look at the wall, and wait for him to whistle me.

[*He remains a moment motionless, then goes out. He comes back immediately, goes to window right, takes up the ladder and carries it out. Pause. HAMM stirs. He yawns under the handkerchief. He removes the handkerchief from his face. Very red face. Black glasses.*]

HAMM: Me – [*he yawns*] – to play. [*He holds the handkerchief spread out before him.*] Old stancher! [*He takes off his glasses, wipes his eyes, his face, the glasses, puts them on again, folds the handkerchief and puts it neatly in the breast-pocket of his dressing-gown. He clears his throat, joins the tips of his fingers.*] Can there be misery – [*he yawns*] – loftier than mine? No doubt. Formerly. But now? [*Pause.*] My father? [*Pause.*] My mother? [*Pause.*] My…dog? [*Pause.*] Oh I am willing to believe they suffer as much as such creatures can suffer. But does that mean their sufferings equal mine? No doubt. [*Pause.*] No, all is a – [*he yawns*] – bsolute, [*proudly*] the bigger a man is the fuller he is. [*Pause. Gloomily.*] And the emptier. [*He sniffs.*] Clov! [*Pause.*] No, alone. [*Pause.*] What dreams! Those forests! [*Pause.*] Enough, it's time it ended, in the refuge, too. [*Pause.*] And yet I hesitate, I hesitate to…to end. Yes, there it is, it's time it ended and yet I hesitate to – [*he yawns*] – to end. [*Yawns.*] God, I'm tired, I'd be better off in bed. [*He whistles. Enter CLOV immediately. He halts beside the chair.*] You pollute the air. [*Pause.*] Get me ready, I'm going to bed.

CLOV: I've just got you up.

HAMM: And what of it?

CLOV: I can't be getting you up and putting you to bed every five minutes, I have things to do.

[*Pause.*]

HAMM: Did you ever see my eyes?

CLOV: No.

HAMM: Did you never have the curiosity, while I was sleeping, to take off my glasses and look at my eyes?

CLOV: Pulling back the lids? [*Pause*] No.

HAMM: One of these days I'll show them to you. [*Pause.*] It seems they've gone all white. [*Pause.*] What time is it?

CLOV: The same as usual.

HAMM: [*Gesture towards window right.*] Have you looked?

CLOV: Yes.

HAMM: Well?

CLOV: Zero.

HAMM: It'd need to rain.

CLOV: It won't rain.

[*Pause.*]

HAMM: Apart from that, how do you feel?

CLOV: I don't complain.

HAMM: You feel normal?

CLOV: [*Irritably.*] I tell you I don't complain!

HAMM: I feel a little queer. [*Pause.*] Clov!

CLOV: Yes.

HAMM: Have you not had enough?

CLOV: Yes! [*Pause.*] Of what?

HAMM: Of this...this...thing?

CLOV: I always had. [*Pause.*] Not you?

HAMM: [*Gloomily.*] Then there's no reason for it to change.

CLOV: It may end. [*Pause.*] All life long the same questions, the same answers.

HAMM: Get me ready. [CLOV *does not move.*] Go and get the sheet.

[CLOV *does not move.*] Clov!

CLOV: Yes.

HAMM: I'll give you nothing more to eat.

CLOV: Then we'll die.

HAMM: I'll give you just enough to keep you from dying. You'll be hungry all the time.

CLOV: Then we shan't die. [*Pause.*] I'll go and get the sheet. [*He goes towards the door.*]

pp5–8, Endgame (Faber, 2006 edn [1958])

Activity 2

Comparing prose and drama

Read Extracts 3 and 4 and answer the following questions.

AO1

1. What is happening in each extract? Identify any themes or concerns.

AOs 1 and 3

2. Compare the subject matter.

AOs 1 and 2

3. What does each extract tell us about the attitudes of the characters – Billy Pilgrim and his daughter Barbara, and Hamm and Clov – towards social norms and accepted ways of behaving?

4. What do you notice about each writer's choice of language and its effect?

AOs 1, 2 and 3

5. Compare how the narrative voices and stage directions deliver the writers' messages.

AOs 1 and 2

6. How does each writer use setting (the planet Tralfamadore and a room with a disappeared view) as a metaphor?

7. What is the effect on the reader of the tone of each extract?

8. Is there any humour to be found in these extracts?

AOs 1, 2 and 3

9. Compare the use of settings, tone and mood in the extracts.

AOs 1, 2, 3 and 4

10. How far do you think these extracts demonstrate typical features of the **dystopia** subgenre?

11. Compare the extracts to any other modern literature you have read that presents a departure from 'mainstream' culture or society, and even a recognisable reality.

12. The science-fiction context in *Slaughterhouse 5* and the absurd alternative reality in *Endgame* can be viewed as products of their time – an obsession with space travel and aliens in the 1950s and 1960s, and a preoccupation with the pointlessness and futility of post-war everyday life. How relevant for you, in the 21st century, is either of these texts and its concerns?

13. Beckett expressed admiration for the human condition and how he was amazed that humanity kept going, despite the trials of life. Examine how he presents this message through Clov and Hamm in this extract. Compare this with how Vonnegut presents Pilgrim's attempts to cope with the trials of life he faces in the extract.

14. You have examined the idea of characters outside a recognisable and acceptable social setting. Is there any use of **realism** in these extracts? (For example, external events and settings, real in the world of the reader – such as the Second World War and the radio – relationships with the media, and a sense of a society 'out there somewhere'.

Key terms

Dystopia a fictional place or society, including imaginary settings, which is damaged, frightening or has stopped functioning.

Realism the presentation of characters, language, setting and plots which reflects the experiences and behaviour of ordinary people and everyday life.

Drama and poetry

Here we compare an extract from the ending of a play and a poem, both published in 2006. They were published in a period that was defined by the aftermath of 9/11, the war on terror and attitudes towards terrorists and terrorism. However, the play is set in 1947 in response to key events of significance at that time, whereas the poem, even though no date is mentioned, strongly suggests the concerns of the world in which it has been written. Despite these differences in the time period of their settings, these texts are examples of social and cultural responses to the horrors of war, partition and divided families, with children as the main victims. These two extracts have an interesting preoccupation with names and the words used to identify people, both as individuals and in social groups.

Pali (later called Altaaf) is a young boy whose family is caught up in the British Partition (separation) of India and Pakistan in 1947. Many Muslim families fled to the newly-created Pakistan and Hindus and Sikhs to the carved-up India. Pali's family, like many others, lost Pali in the chaos of the mass exodus (in fact, the biggest movement of people in recorded history). This scene comes from the penultimate scene of the play where Pali is reunited with his father, Manohar Lal and his mother, Kaushalya. Pali had been taken into a Muslim family and raised as their own son before he was found. His Hindu parents celebrate his home-coming with their neighbours.

> ## Extract 5
> *Child of the Divide* (2006), Sudha Bhuchar
>
> MANOHAR LAL *and their friends are celebrating the return of their son with the singing of a Punjabi festive song.* KAUSHALYA *is resplendent in a red chunri,* PALI *is withdrawn. As the song finishes, a* MAN *and a* WOMAN *congratulate* MANOHAR LAL *and* KAUSHALYA *on* PALI's *return.*
>
> WOMAN Who knows the ways of God? The child you held safely to your bosom was snatched by death and the child who strayed away has come back safe and sound.
> MAN He's a lucky boy indeed to have had God's protection.
> WOMAN He's very quiet.
> KAUSHALYA So much has happened for him.
> *PALI quietly gets his prayer mat, lays it down, and starts to do his namaaz, much to the horror of the guests.*
> WOMAN What's going on, Kaushalya? What is your son doing?
> MANOHAR LAL He instinctively knows when it's time for namaaz [prayer].
> MAN Manohar bhai, we don't want a Muslim amongst us.
> MANOHAR LAL They were very good parents to him. They don't have a child of their own. It was natural for them to bring him up as a Muslim. What else could they do?
> MAN You know what these people are like. They go round converting because it gets them to Heaven. They've taken one of ours. We can't allow this.
> WOMAN Next he'll be asking for meat – will you give it to him?
> MANOHAR LAL Even his tastes will have to change slowly.
> WOMAN Hai Ram! Have you thought, who will give him their girl if word gets out about all this?
> KAUSHALYA I can't worry about his marriage just yet. I still have to win his heart.
> *The* MAN *goes up to* PALI
> MAN What were you doing?

Key terms

9/11 The name given to the destruction of the World Trade Center, or Twin Towers, in New York on 11 September 2001, with two hijacked planes.

War on terror the ongoing military actions of the UK and the US, and initially other European countries, to stamp out Al Qaeda and protect the UK, the US and Europe from terror threats and actions.

PALI I was saying my namaaz.

MAN We won't allow this thing here. From today, no namaaz, you understand?

KAUSHALYA He's only a child, leave him.

MAN Manohar Lal, better call a pandit and a barber. We need to shave his head and make him pure again. Undo this conversion.

MANOHAR LAL All in good time, bhai, let him adjust to his circumstances.

MAN You will regret it if you wait a minute longer.

MANOHAR LAL There's too much emphasis placed on these things.

MAN You don't care that your son has come back as a Muslim?

MANOHAR LAL It is enough for me that my son has come back.

MAN I can't believe my ears. What is your name, boy?

PALI Altaaf.

MAN No, your name is Pali. Who told you your name is Altaaf?

PALI My abbaji [father].

MAN Abbaji. This is your pitaji [father, Hindu]. Repeat your name five times – Pali, Pali…Pali.

MANOHAR LAL Please. I will not let you frighten my boy.

MAN Either sort him out or send him back to those Muslims. We won't tolerate this here. (To WOMAN.) Chalo.

WOMAN Might have been better if he had never been found.

The MAN and WOMAN leave.

MANOHAR LAL (*internal voice*)

I live among them

But these are not my people,

My people

Cared not for Bhagwan or Allah.

They shared

Love and lassi

In each other's homes

What happened, then,

To cause this narrowing of minds

And the broadening of this divide?

PALI I was only doing my prayers.

KAUSHALYA I know, but we pray in a different way. We'll teach you to pray our way and we'll call you Pali again.

PALI But that's not my name.

He starts crying.

MANOHAR LAL Even our hearts are left across the border, beta [child]. This place will never be home.

KAUSHALYA We had to start again and try to belong.

PALI People should belong to each other and not to places.

MANOHAR LAL Yes, you are right, and we are family.

KAUSHALYA When Gudiya was born and you were jealous, you remember you would run to me and lie on my stomach? I would wrap my dupatta [head cover] over you and you would pretend that you were a baby growing inside me. You came from me, beta, and now you've come back to me.

PALI *goes into her arms. The beginning of reconnection.*

Act 2, Scene 9, pp 55–8, *Child of the Divide* (Methuen, 2006)

Extract 6

‘The right word’ (2006), Imtiaz Dharker

Outside the door,
lurking in the shadows,
is a terrorist.

Is that the wrong description?
Outside that door,
taking shelter in the shadows,
is a freedom-fighter.

I haven’t got this right.
Outside, waiting in the shadows,
Is a hostile militant.

Are words no more
than wavering, wavering flags?
Outside your door,
Watchful in the shadows,
is a guerrilla warrior.

God help me.
Outside, defying every shadow,
stands a martyr.
I saw his face.

No words can help me now.
Just outside the door,
lost in shadows,
is a child who looks like mine.

One word for you.
Outside my door,
his hand too steady,
his eyes too hard
is a boy who looks like your son, too.

I open the door.
Come in, I say.
Come in and eat with us.

The child steps in
and carefully, at my door,
takes off his shoes.

pp25–26, *The Terrorist at My Table* (Penguin Poetry, 2007 edn [2006])

Further reading

To connect with Extracts 5 and 6, on children in modern war and conflict:

- ‘School Among the Ruins’ (2004), Adrienne Rich – poetry
- *The Kite Runner* (2003), Khaled Hosseini – a novel.

To connect with Extract 5 on presentations of post-partition India, being Indian and cultural division and diversity:

- ‘Our Town with the Whole of India!’ (2007), Daljit Nagra – poetry
- *The God of Small Things* (1997), Arundhati Roy – a novel.

To connect with the human cost of terrorism since 9/11, with opposite viewpoints and voices:

- ‘Out of the Blue’ (2008), Simon Armitage – poetry
- ‘The terrorist at my table’ (2006), Imtiaz Dharker – poetry
- *Decade* (2011) – a collection of perspectives by 20 playwrights (drama)
- *Falling Man* (2007), Don DeLillo – novel.

Activity 3

Comparing drama and poetry

Read Extracts 5 and 6 and answer the following questions.

AO1

1. What is happening in each extract?

2. Identify any themes and messages.

AOs 1 and 3

3. Compare the subject matter.

AOs 1 and 2

4. Identify the characters and speaker in the extracts. How are they described?

AOs 1, 2 and 3

5. Compare how the boys are presented.

6. Compare the importance of names and naming in the texts.

7. Compare the language use in the extracts. Examine how the writers use repetition, emotive language and questions.

8. Compare the use of dialogue in the play with the conversational style, direct speech and direct address in the poem.

9. The forms are very different, but the mood, tone and setting have many similarities. Compare ways in which each genre is used to create those similarities.

AOs 1, 2, 3, and 4

10. Compare how the writers communicate their attitudes towards the events and characters they each present.

11. Both extracts are from 2006. Identify and evaluate any shared contexts in the texts that help you to make connections between them. Is there any way to pinpoint Extract 5 as a 21st-century text?

12. If you are studying either of these texts to explore any same-period different-genre comparisons, examine any connections you find between them and one of the suggested texts for Further reading.

All three genres

So far in this chapter, you have compared every combination of two genres of the same period.

The most challenging task is to compare all three genres across the same period. It is challenging in three ways:

- structure – organising your comparisons
- relevance – focusing on the question
- priorities – prioritising your comparisons.

Structure

You have to juggle three texts in your analysis without repetition and with decent coverage of them all. This is significantly more difficult than comparing two, which is a balancing act, but not a juggle in the same way.

The least effective way to make a comparative analysis of three or more texts is to spend half the time on the first text, half the time on comparing the second text with the first text and no time at all on the remaining texts. This method is the most common pitfall of A Level essays, even in coursework. Structuring your comparison is a key to the success of your analysis of three or more texts. Follow the guidance given so far and find similarities to uncover differences. Tackle the comparison by common features of the texts. Subject matter is the best place to begin: plot, themes and ideas. Identify how they can be linked through their 'typicality' within the period: concerns, messages and movements. This might be based on shared macro and/or literary contexts. You have then begun to address AOs 1 and 4. You can move into the use of technique to tackle AO2 and analyse connections between the uses and effects of style: language, form and structure, tone, mood, setting and characterisation – in other words, the same literary analysis you have been doing since Chapter 1 and throughout your course of literary study.

Relevance
Always focus on the question. You might have more to say than the question asks for. If you veer off task, even if your structure is sound, your analysis can become irrelevant and the comparisons you make will be lost on the reader. This pitfall is the case when you study just one text. It is three times worse if you are writing about three.

Priorities
You have to prioritise. Choose which areas you want to cover and make points that demonstrate the argument you are proposing. The argument should always be: 'What connects all these texts in time and why do they belong together in this essay?' You cannot cover everything, even if you focus on the question – not even in an extended coursework essay, and certainly not in a timed examination. It might seem frustrating that you know more about your texts than you can usefully explore in a three-way comparison. However, if you prioritise, you can cover a few areas for comparative analysis with useful and interesting detail, evidence and exploration, however many texts you cover. If you do not prioritise, you will most likely skate over the kind of detail that comes with evidence. You might then make random, assertive points that lack a decent sequence or logic and veer off the question or deal with it superficially. Either is bad news for good marks.

Checking over your response
Once you have a structured, relevant and prioritised plan for your comparative analysis, you can refine it. Check that your structure is easy to follow, that all your comparisons really do answer the question and that all your texts get the coverage they need.

Similarities and differences across three genres
You will find more differences than similarities when you compare texts across the three genres. The varieties of genre and the techniques used to work with the genre conventions are bound to create more differences than you can manage to explore in one essay. Do not force the comparison. They are written in different genres for a reason. The writers have chosen the forms because they best express how each one wants to send their messages out to you, the reader and/or the audience. Follow the guidance you have already been given: start with the subject matter and go on to context, period and then technique. Examine what is typical about your texts from the same period across the three genres.

Now look at how comparison of three genres works in practice.

> ### Examiner's tip
>
> **Prioritising your comparisons**
> Whoever marks your work can see if you know how to prioritise.
>
> You are rewarded for your confident and appropriate selection of material to compare. You are not punished because you did not cover everything that has ever been thought about the texts you are comparing.

The following poem is the title poem from *The School Among the Ruins* by the American poet Adrienne Rich. Rich has publicly condemned the war on terror and this poem is a graphic documentary of that condemnation. It is based on real events of recent bombing campaigns, from the Balkans to the Middle East. She attempts to give a voice to the vulnerable during wartime, in this case children.

In '1', the first section, Rich begins with a universal description of a typical school day. In '2', she moves to a specific narrative style to tell the story of the attack. '3' to '6' explore the impact of this event on the school, the children and the teachers. '7' versifies the actual news report of the events at the time.

Extract 7
'The School Among the Ruins' (2001), Adrienne Rich

Beirut.Baghdad.Sarajevo.Bethlehem.Kabul. Not of course here.

1
Teaching the first lesson and the last
– great falling light of summer will you last
longer than schooltime?
When children flow
in columns at the doors
BOYS GIRLS and the busy teachers

open or close high windows
with hooked poles drawing darkgreen shades

closets unlocked, locked
questions unasked, asked, when
love of the fresh impeccable
sharp-pencilled yes
order without cruelty

a street on earth neither heaven nor hell
busy with commerce and worship
young teachers walking to school

fresh bread and early-open foodstalls

2
When the offensive rocks the sky when nightglare
misconstrues day and night when lived-in
rooms from the upper city
tumble cratering lower streets

cornices of olden ornament human debris
when fear vacuums out the streets

When the whole town flinches
blood on the undersole thickening to glass

Whoever crosses hunched knees bent a contested zone
knows why she does this suicidal thing

School's now in session day and night
children sleep
in the classrooms teachers rolled close

3
How the good teacher loved
his school the students
the lunchroom with fresh sandwiches

lemonade and milk
the classroom glass cages
of moss and turtles
teaching responsibility

A morning breaks without bread or fresh-poured milk
parents or lesson plans

diarrhea first question of the day
children shivering it's September
Second question: where is my mother?

4
One: I don't know where your mother
is Two: I don't know
why they are trying to hurt us
Three: or the latitude and longitude
of their hatred Four: I don't know if we
hate them as much I think there's more toilet paper
in the supply closet I'm going to break it open

Today this is your lesson:
write as clearly as you can
your name home street and number
down on this page
No you can't go home yet
but you aren't lost
this is our school

I'm not sure what we'll eat
we'll look for healthy roots and greens
searching for water though the pipes are broken

5
There's a young cat sticking
her head through window bars
she's hungry like us
but can feed on mice
her bronze erupting fur
speaks of a life already wild

her golden eyes
don't give quarter She'll teach us Let's call her
Sister
when we get milk we'll give her some

6
I've told you, let's try to sleep in this funny camp
All night pitiless pilotless things go shrieking
above us to somewhere

Don't let your faces turn to stone
Don't stop asking me why
Let's pay attention to our cat she needs us

Maybe tomorrow the bakers can fix their ovens

7
"We sang them to naps told stories made
shadow animals with our hands

wiped human debris off boots and coats
sat learning by heart the names
some were too young to write
some had forgotten how"

pp22–5, *The School Among the Ruins* (Norton, 2005 edn [2001])

Activity 4

Comparing all three genres

Read Extract 5 from *Child of the Divide* in this chapter again, and Extract 5 from *The Kite Runner* in Chapter 4. Then read Extract 7 below.

AO1

1. Identify what is happening and any themes in Extract 7. Refer to the notes you made on what is happening and any themes in the other texts.

AOs 1 and 3

2. Identify similarities in the subject matter of the three texts.

AOs 1 and 2

3. Examine the presentations of children across the texts.

AOs 1, 2, 3 and 4

4. Which characters are you encouraged to like/dislike in each extract? How does each writer create this response in you? Examine the tone, the use of names, the activities of the children and the settings.

5. Compare where your sympathies lie.

6. Identify any typicalities of the period: ways in which these texts are written that reflect the period of publication. Identify and evaluate which contexts influence what you have learned about the texts from these extracts.

7. If you are studying a group of texts from the same period across all the genres, do questions 2, 4, 5 and 6. Adapt question 3 to examine the presentation of what is important in your own texts.

Summary

This chapter has introduced you to comparing texts from the same period across different genres. You should now be able to identify similarities and differences and do a comparative analysis of a range of same-period examples of:

- poetry and prose
- prose and drama
- drama and poetry
- all three genres.

7   Different genre, different period

Finding similarities and differences

Comparing texts and extracts across genre and time is another of the more challenging ways to analyse your texts. The differences and contrasts will inevitably be greater than the previous comparisons you have considered in Chapters 4–6. Despite the many differences you are bound to uncover, there can still be many similarities between your cross-genre, cross-period texts. You can make meaningful connections by following the same guidelines that you have been given so far: address the AOs and look for what the texts have in common.

Subject matter

Subject matter is the best place to start because what a text is about does not rely on the period or style in which it is written. Stories, narratives, thoughts and feelings about the human condition and how we have lived, loved and died throughout time can often be connected. This aspect of our common humanity leads to what was described earlier in Chapter 1 as the universal themes of literature, such as jealousy, revenge or hope.

Contexts

Of course, you might find that the texts express concerns, tell stories or present characters that emerge from their particular era and the social, cultural and political considerations of their time. These aspects of the texts might be bound by the contexts of the period, possibly the macro and/or the literary influences on the texts. Even here, there might be similarity as well as difference – concerns and how they are expressed can come around more than once in history. After all, people still go to war, try to get rich, kill each other to get what they want, protect their children, and sacrifice themselves for others. We still challenge these social norms by passive resistance to fighting, vows of poverty and chastity, abuse of those in our care, and so on. Even where our societies and values seem to have changed, identifying something about humanity and what makes us human across time often sparks the connections you can make between your texts. It might also trigger your own response to the ideas and emotions that the texts suggest.

Additionally, a text from a later time can revive the traditions of an earlier time, so some literary contexts might be similar. These texts are often from the same genre, such as the ways in which the Elizabethan and Jacobean dramatists developed traditions and techniques based on Greek and Roman classical models. Sometimes a literary tradition revived from an earlier era can also work across genres. For example, the borrowing of classical models or subject matter from classical mythology, originally expressed in drama, has not only influenced playwriting in later times. Classical models also influence the poetry and prose of 20th-century Modernist works, such as *The Wasteland* by the American poet T.S. Eliot and *Ulysses* by the Irish novelist James Joyce. The structure for Joyce's novel – a day in the life of Jewish Dubliner, Lionel Bloom – is based in Homer's epic poem *The Odyssey*, about the archetypal wanderer. Both Eliot and Joyce published their texts in 1922, and both became hugely influential on post-war fiction.

Technique

It is also possible to approach your comparison through the styles that the writers use, and analyse the ways in which they use techniques and subgenres. You can compare your texts through the ways in which they:

- tell a tale

- explore or symbolise emotions

- present a place or mood

- use language to create that tale

- show how their characters or speakers talk and who they talk to.

You might find some similar use of conventions and techniques that are shared across both genres and periods. You might also find that the individual handling of technique in each of your texts produces some interesting differences.

Let us consider some examples of these connections across time and genre in your texts.

Some examples

Connecting Gothic elements: violence, victims and villains

Definition

Gothic literature developed as a branch of romance literature in the 18th century. Its early influence can be seen in novels such as *Northanger Abbey* by Jane Austen. (The novel was not published until 1817, but it was written at the end of the 18th century.) The Gothic subgenre and style also contains macabre aspects of a horror subgenre explored in novels such as *Frankenstein* (1818) by Mary Shelley. This novel reflects the 19th-century fascination with science, death and the supernatural. In the 20th century, Angela Carter's short story collection, *The Bloody Chamber*, features supernatural, fantasy or unwelcoming settings and updated, rewritten fairy tales. It features modern 'Gothic' elements that combine the dark elements within human nature with an exploration of sexuality, especially female.

Texts published even earlier than the 18th century that contain elements of the macabre and dark sexuality can still be said to have Gothic elements. Examples include Elizabethan and Jacobean dramas, such as *Doctor Faustus* and *The White Devil*, with their preoccupation with damnation, death and violence, and the 17th-century poet John Milton, with his depictions of hell in *Paradise Lost*.

Gothic elements

If you are comparing a range of texts because they are said to have some Gothic elements, what are you looking for and what features might you find?

- A deal with the devil and/or the presence of the supernatural.

- A depiction of religious, usually Christian, values.

- Violence and/or (often gruesome) death and a fascination with these.

- Depictions of a medieval world or/and the classical past.

- Recurring motifs (symbols), such as blood.

- Night-time settings and/or a mood of fear and suspense.

- Presentation of sensational acts and behaviour and/or strong emotions.
- Explorations of sexuality and/or the dark side of human nature.
- A preoccupation with the human states of isolation, imprisonment and/or excessive power.
- The breaking of social and moral conventions and codes.

You do not have to focus on Gothic elements in your texts to consider how these features can help you to compare your own texts. For example, revisit these extracts:

- Chapter 4, Extracts 7 and 8, from the plays *The White Devil* (1609–12) and *Doctor Faustus* (1594)
- Chapter 5, Extracts 5 and 6, from the novel *Wuthering Heights* (1847) and the short story 'The Bloody Chamber' (1979).

Activity 4 in Chapter 4 and Activity 3 in Chapter 5 showed you how to make connections with texts of the same genre within the same period and then across periods. You might have connected the broody or frank presentation of impending violence in the plot, themes, tone and mood. You might have shown how violence is suggested through the ways in which the language and setting are used. You might have noted the threat of violence, its effects on the reader or audience member and where your sympathies lay. You might have identified characters as innocents or victims. Were they presented as naive? Foolish? Subservient? Did you identify any chilling, demonic or corrupt perpetrators? Was there any irony in these presentations? For example, the perpetrator in *The White Devil* is a high-ranking churchman. If you know the play, you might know that his victim, Flamineo, is himself a murderer, a villain – you could say a perpetrator – in other scenes from the play.

You can use what you have already discovered to expand your connections to all four extracts. For example, are these four extracts above equally complex in their character roles as that of Flamineo? You could consider how violence and villainy leads to premature death in all these texts. However, while death swirls around every character in *Wuthering Heights*, there are no actual murderers anywhere in the novel. By contrast, very few characters in *The White Devil* do not commit a murder.

Look at how all the texts have sexual elements in their plots and themes, but in these particulars extracts, sexual elements are only presented in 'The Bloody Chamber'. Sex and violence are closely linked in this text. If you are studying the others, would you say that was true of them also? How are they linked? For example, in 'The Bloody Chamber', the victim is often placed in settings with sexual connotations: bedrooms, beds, night-time, darkness. These are examples of recurring motifs, and their presence prepares us for her intended final setting: a coffin next to the coffins of the previous newly-wed wives. Other settings and motifs suggest the sexual tension in the story: the speeding train, the restless waves, flickering candles, the heavy perfumes of flowers, cigars and scented wood. Is sex presented as an important theme, using techniques such as motifs and symbols, in any of the other three texts? How?

These are examples of some of the ways you can start to develop your cross-genre, cross-period texts. You will find that the exploration of sex, violence, death and murder are universal themes which can connect texts in several ways.

Connecting supernatural elements

Texts with Gothic elements are likely to have some supernatural elements. You can compare how the previous four extracts above (and the texts from which they come) might use the supernatural. If you add to this comparison Shakespeare's play *Macbeth* (1606), Mary Shelley's novel *Frankenstein* (1818), and John Milton's long narrative poem *Paradise Lost* (1667), you will soon uncover connections based on supernatural, ungodly and hellish elements. You will also find connections between sexual elements in each of these texts. They are very different from the sexual elements in the extracts we considered as 'Gothic' even though these texts can also be said to have Gothic elements. These three texts are more interesting in the way they present sexuality as shameful, repressed or emasculating. If you study any of them, it is worth comparing their presentations of sex and attitudes towards sexual relationships. In Extracts 1, 2 and 3 later in this chapter, you can investigate connections between these three texts and how any of them connect with the four you have considered above.

Connecting pastoral elements: nature, lightness and darkness

If you compare texts for their pastoral elements, what are you looking for and what features might you find?

- A rural, natural setting: often in English countryside, gardens, farmland or forests.
- Sometimes the natural setting or rural community is set in contrast with an urban setting or community.
- Characters are shaped by their strong connections with nature and the natural world.
- A rustic way of life: simple, traditional lifestyles and characters are presented at odds with an industrial or mechanical world.
- A paradise: rural life is often presented in an idealised way.
- Innocence: characters are often presented as pure and innocent, particularly children. Sometimes the loss of innocence and the Fall of Paradise is presented.
- Subject matter about love, especially romantic love, and its development between the main characters, in the plot and themes.
- Sex and sexuality are seen as natural and positive aspects of human nature.

Even if you are not looking for specifically 'pastoral elements', you might find that these features provide a useful connection between your texts. For example, revisit these extracts:

- Chapter 5, Extracts 7 and 8, from the plays *As You Like It* (c.1599) and *Arcadia* (1993)
- Chapter 5, Extracts 1 and 2, the poems 'Nurse's Song' (c.1789) and 'Rain' (2010).

There are clear links between *As You Like it* and *Arcadia* in that they feature a playful and comic approach to sex and sexual relationships, presenting this aspect of human behaviour as natural and inevitable. This is very different from how sex is presented in the texts which have 'Gothic' links. The two poems above are not interested in sexual relationships. They are concerned with parental relationships, the ways in which children are seen, and their relationships with each other and the natural world. There are connections between all four texts here though. The carefree attitude of the children in the poems and the lightness of tone in their presentation are similar to the light presentation of sexual relationships in the two plays. All the behaviours are seen as natural and inevitable in these four extracts. While the drama extracts are less concerned with the environment and nature, the plays they come from are set largely in a forest or garden. They explore ideas about the forest as a world apart and about human interference in nature through gardening. If you are studying any of these texts, consider how they can be connected through the ways in which they debate concerns about where people fit into nature. Consider the writers' messages about human nature and 'natural' behaviour.

It is also interesting to look at how they differ from other texts which use the natural world as a key setting and symbol. For example, why would we consider *Macbeth* and *Wuthering Heights* to have Gothic and not pastoral elements? Macbeth is out on a heath, while the characters of *Wuthering Heights* move between moorland and manicured gardens. What is different about these settings and the presentation of the natural world in these texts? These texts also explore sexual relationships, innocent children and romantic love. What is different about the ways in which these elements develop in the Gothic texts which mean that they do not really belong in a pastoral tradition?

William Blake presents pastoral concerns of innocence and loss of innocence using images of the natural world in his poetry collection, *Songs of Innocence and of Experience* (1794). You can explore these connections later in the chapter in Extract 4, with his two short poems 'The Lamb' (1789) and 'The Sick Rose' (1794), and link them to Extract 5, from the novel *Tess of the d'Urbervilles* (1891) by Thomas Hardy.

You might wonder what is pastoral about the usually darker elements of blood and sexual predators that you find in this novel. Its pastoral elements are found in Hardy's concerns, themes and messages about a lost rural life: the innocent girl, the fruitfulness of nature, the superstitious and judgemental way of traditional rural living. You could even say that the heroine, Tess, goes symbolically from the little lamb to the sick rose that concerned Blake a hundred years earlier.

Connecting elements of love
The shared topic of love in all its aspects is an important connection between texts of every genre and subgenre through the ages. For example, the novel *Tess of the d'Urbervilles* belongs to the tradition we call the literature of love, a love story, even though it has several other elements. Another example is the poem 'To His Coy Mistress' (*c.*1640s–1650s) by Andrew Marvell. This is a poem in the metaphysical tradition which is a feature or poetic subgenre of the period from which it comes, the mid 17th century. It is also a widely read love poem, with some attitudes about love

Think about it

Comparing settings as symbols
Is a natural setting, such as a garden or a forest, used as a nurturing escape to transport the characters from their own reality? Consider ways in which harsh landscapes, such as mountains, moorlands and heaths, are used. Are they presented as warnings, or as punishments for the characters, to pay for their sins?

Think about it

Connecting ideas about innocence and experience
These ideas are explored by Blake. Can you compare any other texts you study with pastoral ideas about innocence and experience or worldliness?

Key term

Metaphysical intellectual poetry, usually from 17th-century England. More interested in analysing feelings than expressing them.

and seduction that you might consider to be dependent on the social and literary contexts of its period. Some of its messages and themes about love would be considered universal, and as relevant today as they were when it was written. In this way, it speaks to the reader as an example of a poem about feelings and desires, regardless of when it was written.

Later in the chapter, you can make some interesting contrasts and comparisons between Hardy's novel (Extract 5) and Marvell's poem (Extract 6). See what connections you can make between how these texts present the attempts at seduction of a virgin. Look at how attitudes to time in the Marvell poem differ from the ways in which Shakespeare writes about the relationship between romantic love and time in his Sonnet 116 (1609), in Extract 7. You can make links between how the Shakespeare sonnet presents time as a factor in love with the love poem 'Funeral Blues' (1938) by W.H. Auden (Extract 8), which is a sort of elegy. Both these poetic forms are typically used for love poetry, but it is the meditations on time that link these poems.

> ### Key term
>
> **Elegy** a poem of serious reflection, usually a lament for the dead.

So far, these texts about love focus on persuading someone into sex, loving or otherwise, and the constancy of love over time, both as a theoretical idea and in the face of loss. You can also look at different explorations of how love is linked to loss: lovers doomed to be separated by social status and/or the capricious desires of one of the lovers to change their social status or their status within the relationship. Three examples of love and loss are found in the novels *The God of Small Things* (1997) by Arundhati Roy, the novel *Wuthering Heights*, which we have already discussed, and Shakespeare's play *Antony and Cleopatra* (c.1606). These texts, as examples of love stories, all debate the power of love to conquer space, time, distance and death. Happiness, or at least any lasting happiness, seems to come low on the agenda. If you study any of these texts, consider why that might be the case, if you agree that it is so. You can also link Roy's novel in Extract 9 with the earlier extracts of texts about love, and consider how time affects love, or how love affects time.

No obvious connections?

What about texts without a common subgenre, set of elements or obvious theme, and only the 'pre-1800' period to link them, which could span 450 years? For example, how can you connect the Milton poem in Extract 3, or Blake's poems in Extract 4, with Webster's play *The White Devil* in Chapter 4, or another Jacobean play, John Ford's *'Tis Pity She's a Whore* (1629–33)? One way is to follow the advice about starting with subject matter, particularly the exploration of universal themes, and, if they are there, presentations of character. For example, Milton's poem of 1667 has echoes of Ford's play. They both take the approach of presenting a 'fallen woman' as responsible for the fall of the society within the world of the text. In Ford's case that is the heroine, the 'whore' of the title, Annabella. In Milton's case it is Eve – the original woman and the original fall, on which all women and all falls involving the temptation of man, sexual desire and images of the temptress have since been based, throughout literature and mythology. The idea of the 'fall' also connects the themes and concerns of these texts, as they both explore ideas about the shift from human innocence to experience. The concern with human innocence and experience links with the Blake poems and his concerns over 100 years later. Blake is perhaps less interested in who is to blame and more concerned with who suffers, as 'The Sick Rose' shows.

So far, we have considered ways in which you can link texts from across genres and periods, whichever course or examination you undertake. Look at how your range of connections could be assessed in the examination questions below.

Approaching examination questions

Here are examples of examination questions from A2 papers in 2012.

Reading examination questions

Look at what they ask and how they ask you to make connections between your texts. It is likely to be either the exploration or **critical discussion** (AO3) of how your texts present a **universal theme** (AO1) or the use of a **specific technique** (AO2) (in addition to a general reference to the 'ways' or 'presentation' of an 'idea'). They could include a **named context, area of typicality or a subgenre** (AO4), such as the Gothic, the pastoral, love, the Victorians, the First World War or the struggle for identity in modern literature (in addition to any general instruction to be aware that they have been written at different times or to consider contexts).

> ## Either
> AQA B:
> To what extent do you agree with the view that **pastoral writing** always celebrates the **freedom of a childhood state**?
> [Focus on a theme]

> ## or
> **Gothic literature** demonstrates the **consequences** of disrupting the natural order of things.
> [Focus on a theme]

> ## or
> OCR:
> 'There is a fine line between heroism and foolishness'.
> **In the light of this view**, consider ways in which writers present **heroism**. In your answer, compare one drama text and one poetry text from the above lists.
> [Focus on a theme]

> ## or
> Edexcel:
> 'The varied presentation of the **loss or lack of innocence** of one kind or another is a strong connecting thread between many works of literature.' **How far do you agree with this statement**? In your response you should comment on and analyse the connections and comparisons between at least two texts you have studied.
> You must ensure that at least one text is a post-1990 text, as indicated by * in the list above.
> Note that you should demonstrate what it means to be considering texts as a modern reader, in a modern context and that other readers at other times may well have had other responses.
> [Focus on a theme]

or

Edexcel:

'Because works of literature surprise, exaggerate and subvert expectations, they have the knack of changing the very way in which we look at the world.'

How far do you agree with this statement? In your response you should comment on and analyse the connections and comparisons between at least two texts you have studied.

You must ensure that at least one text is a post-1990 text, as indicated by * in the list above.

Note that you should demonstrate what it means to be considering texts as a modern reader, in a modern context and that other readers at other times may well have had other responses.

[Focus on technique: mood, description, narration and imagery, effects on reader/s]

or

AQA B:

'Gothic writing lacks tension and suspense because the end is always inevitable.'

To what extent do you agree that gothic writing does lack tension and suspense?

[Focus on technique: narrative or dramatic structure and mood]

or

'The countryside may be beautiful but it should also be useful.'

Consider the ways in which the countryside is presented in pastoral writing in the light of this comment.

[Focus on technique: setting]

or

OCR:

'Words can entice us, can compel us, can ensnare us.'

In the light of this view, consider ways in which writers present persuasive or seductive uses of language. In your answer, compare one drama text and one poetry text from the above lists.

[Focus on technique: language use]

Critical analysis (AO3)

All these are examples of questions that focus on ideas because they are all looking for critical analysis (AO3) as well as comparative analysis. How much weight you give to the debate will be determined by how much weight the exam board gives to that part of AO3: the interpretation of views – yours and other people's.

Examiner's tip

Making connections can vary

Look at how readings of a single text can change *depending on their grouping with other similar texts.* Themes and subgenres can represent different focuses for comparison and sharing connections. In one grouping it can be love, in another war, in another Gothic, in another pastoral, in another Victorian – or several at once.

Think about the useful connections you can make. Be open, but stay focused on how you want to link the texts.

Activity 1

Applying a comparative analysis to examination questions

Choose a question from those presented on the previous pages from the examination board whose course you are following. Write a plan that addresses the key words and Assessment Objectives. Use the advice about comparative analysis that you have been given earlier in this chapter.

Extracts and activities

Activity 2

Making connections across period and genre

You have considered a range of ways to perform a cross-genre, cross-period analysis of your texts and applied what you have learned to a typical examination question.

1. Now read the extracts below and choose three from at least two different genres and two different periods. If none of your texts are in the list below, you can substitute one choice for one of your texts if you wish.

2. Make notes on their similarities and differences. Identify any connections between the three that you observe, in their choices of subject matter (AO1), the use of techniques (AO2) and any shared contexts (AO4).

3. Now choose a maximum of three of your own texts that you are studying for comparison. Select an extract of approximately two or three pages if it is prose novel or a play written in prose. If it is a play written in verse or blank verse, such as one by Shakespeare, select approximately 50 lines. If it is an extract from a longer poem, such as Milton's *Paradise Lost*, select approximately 30 lines. Then select a maximum of two texts from the extracts below that you did not examine in question 1. You should have selected a total of three or four extracts to compare.

4. Now do question 2 for your question 3 selections.

In this extract from Shakespeare's *Macbeth*, the Witches go on the heath to meet Macbeth, a thane (Scottish lord), and prophesy his destiny – to become the Thane of Cawdor then King of Scotland.

Extract 1
Macbeth (1606), Shakespeare
Thunder. Enter the three WITCHES

FIRST WITCH
Where hast thou been, sister?

SECOND WITCH
Killing swine.

THIRD WITCH
Sister, where thou?

FIRST WITCH
A sailor's wife had chestnuts in her lap
And munch'd, and munch'd, and munch'd:– 'Give me,' quoth I.
'Aroint thee, witch!' the rump-fed runnion cries.
Her husband's to Aleppo gone, master o' th' Tiger:
But in a sieve I'll thither sail,
And, like a rat without a tail,
I'll do, I'll do, and I'll do.

SECOND WITCH
I'll give thee a wind.

FIRST WITCH
Thou'rt kind.

THIRD WITCH
And I another.

FIRST WITCH
I myself have all the other,
And the very ports they blow,
All the quarters that they know
I' th' shipman's card.
I will drain him dry as hay:
Sleep shall neither night nor day
Hang upon his penthouse lid;
He shall live a man forbid.
Weary sennights nine times nine
Shall he dwindle, peak and pine.
Though his bark cannot be lost,
Yet it shall be tempest-tossed.
Look what I have.

SECOND WITCH
    Show me, show me.

FIRST WITCH
Here I have a pilot's thumb,
Wreck'd as homeward he did come.

Drum within

THIRD WITCH
A drum, a drum;
Macbeth doth come.

ALL
The Weird Sisters, hand in hand,
Posters of the sea and land,
Thus do go about, about,
Thrice to thine and thrice to mine,
And thrice again, to make up nine.
Peace, the charm's wound up.

Enter MACBETH *and* BANQUO

MACBETH
So foul and fair a day I have not seen.

BANQUO
How far is't call'd to Forres? What are these,
So withered and so wild in their attire,
That look not like the inhabitants o' th'earth,
And yet are on't? Live you? or are you aught
That man may question? You seem to understand me,
By each at once her chappy finger laying
Upon her skinny lips: you should be women,
And yet your beards forbid me to interpret
That you are so.

MACBETH Speak, if you can: what are you?

FIRST WITCH
All hail, Macbeth, hail to thee, Thane of Glamis.

SECOND WITCH
All hail, Macbeth, hail to thee, Thane of Cawdor.

THIRD WITCH
All hail, Macbeth, thou shalt be King hereafter.

Act 1, Scene 3, Lines 1–47, *Shakespeare*, New Cambridge Shakespeare, 2008 edn [1606]

(Cambridge University Press)

The following extract comes about halfway through the novel. Frankenstein has fled into the mountains, from civilisation, from his family, from the creature and the consequences of his actions. However, the creature catches up with him, and this is their first confrontation since Frankenstein abandoned his creation.

Extract 2
Frankenstein (1818), Mary Shelley

It was nearly noon when I arrived at the top of the ascent. For some time I sat upon the rock that overlooks the sea of ice. A mist covered both that and the surrounding mountains. Presently a breeze dissipated the cloud, and I descended upon the glacier. The surface is very uneven, rising like the waves of a troubled sea, descending low, and interspersed by rifts that sink deep. The field of ice is almost a league in width, but I spent nearly two hours in crossing it. The opposite mountain is a bare perpendicular rock. From the side where I now stood Montanvert was exactly opposite, at the distance of a league; and above it rose Mont Blanc, in awful majesty. I remained in a recess of the rock, gazing on this wonderful and stupendous scene. The sea, or rather the vast river of ice, wound among its dependent mountains, whose aerial summits hung over its recesses. Their icy and glittering peaks shone in the sunlight over the clouds. My heart, which was before sorrowful, now swelled with something like joy; I exclaimed, 'Wandering spirits, if indeed ye wander, and do not rest in your narrow beds, allow me this faint happiness, or take me, as your companion, away from the joys of life.'

As I said this I suddenly beheld the figure of a man, at some distance, advancing towards me with superhuman speed. He bounded over the crevices in the ice, among which I had walked with caution; his stature, also, as he approached, seemed to exceed that of man. I was troubled; a mist came over my eyes, and I felt a faintness seize me, but I was quickly restored by the cold gale of the mountains. I perceived, as the shape came nearer (sight tremendous and abhorred!) that it was the wretch whom I had created. I trembled with rage and horror, resolving to wait his approach and then close with him in mortal combat. He approached; his countenance bespoke bitter anguish, combined with disdain and malignity, while its unearthly ugliness rendered it almost too horrible for human eyes. But I scarcely observed this; rage and

Did you know?

Intertextuality in *Frankenstein* and *Paradise Lost*
Frankenstein has as its epigraph a quotation from Milton's *Paradise Lost*, Book X, lines 743–5: 'Did I request thee, Maker, from my clay / To mould Me man? Did I solicit thee / From Darkness to promote me?'

Key term

Epigraph a quotation on the title page of a book or under the title of a poem.

hatred had at first deprived me of utterance, and I recovered only to overwhelm him with words expressive of furious detestation and contempt.

'Devil,' I exclaimed, 'do you dare approach me? And do not you fear the fierce vengeance of my arm wreaked on your miserable head? Begone, vile insect! Or rather, stay, that I may trample you to dust! And, oh! That I could, with the extinction of your miserable existence, restore those victims whom you have so diabolically murdered!'

'I expected this reception,' said the daemon. 'All men hate the wretched; how, then, must I be hated, who am miserable beyond all living things! Yet you, my creator, detest and spurn me, thy creature, to whom thou art bound by ties only dissoluble by the annihilation of one of us. You purpose to kill me. How dare you sport thus with life? Do your duty towards me, and I will do mine towards you and the rest of mankind. If you will comply with my conditions, I will leave them and you at peace; but if you refuse, I will glut the maw of death, until it be satiated with the blood of your remaining friends.'

'Abhorred monster! Fiend that thou art! The tortures of hell are too mild a vengeance for thy crimes. Wretched devil! You reproach me with your creation, come on, then, that I may extinguish the spark which I so negligently bestowed.'

My rage was without bounds; I sprang on him, impelled by all the feelings which can arm one being against the existence of another.

He easily eluded me and said—

'Be calm! I entreat you to hear me before you give vent to your hatred on my devoted head. Have I not suffered enough, that you seek to increase my misery? Life, although it may only be an accumulation of anguish, is dear to me, and I will defend it. Remember, thou hast made me more powerful than thyself; my height is superior to thine, my joints more supple. But I will not be tempted to set myself in opposition to thee. I am thy creature, and I will be even mild and docile to my natural lord and king if thou wilt also perform thy part, the which thou owest me. Oh, Frankenstein, be not equitable to every other and trample upon me alone, to whom thy justice, and even thy clemency and affection, is most due. Remember that I am thy creature;

I ought to be thy Adam, but I am rather the fallen angel, whom thou drivest from joy for no misdeed. Everywhere I see bliss, from which I alone am irrevocably excluded. I was benevolent and good; misery made me a fiend. Make me happy, and I shall again be virtuous.'

'Begone! I will not hear you. There can be no community between you and me; we are enemies. Begone, or let us try our strength in a fight, in which one must fall.'

pp76–78, *Frankenstein* (Wordsworth Classics, 1999 edn [1818])

Extract 3 is from Book IX, after God has cast Adam and Eve out of the Garden
of Eden for eating the forbidden fruit after temptation by the serpent.

Extract 3
Paradise Lost (1667), John Milton

No more of talk where God or Angel guest
With Man, as with his friend, familiar us'd,
To sit indulgent, and with him partake
Rural repast; permitting him the while
Venial discourse unblam'd. I now must change
Those notes to tragick; foul distrust, and breach
Disloyal on the part of Man, revolt,
And disobedience: on the part of Heaven
Now alienated, distance and distaste,
Anger and just rebuke, and judgement given,
That brought into this world a world of woe,

Sin and her shadow Death, and Misery
Death's harbinger: Sad talk! yet argument
Not less but more heroick than the wrath
Of stern Achilles on his foe pursued
Thrice fugitive about Troy wall; or rage
Of Turnus for Lavinia disespous'd;
Or Neptune's ire, or Juno's, that so long
Perplexed the Greek, and Cytherea's son…

Lines 1–19, *Paradise Lost*, Book IX

The first poem in Extract 4 is from the 'Innocence' section of William Blake's
Songs of Innocence and of Experience, and the second poem is from the
'Experience' section. Blake's subtitle is 'contrary states of the human soul'.
Each of the poems deals with ideas, subject matter, symbols and form in
ways that are typical of the poems in their section. The poem 'Nurse's Song'
(Extract 1 from Chapter 5) is also from the 'Innocence' section.

Extract 4
'The Lamb' (1789), William Blake

Little Lamb who made thee?
Dost thou Know who made thee
  Gave thee life and bid thee feed
  By the stream and ofer the mead;
  Gave thee clothing of delight,
  Softest clothing wooly bright;
  Gave thee such a tender voice,
  Making all the vales rejoice.
Little Lamb who made thee?
Dost thou know who made thee?

Little Lamb I'll tell thee,
Little Lamb I'll tell thee:
  He is called by thy name,
  For he calls himself a Lamb.
  He is meek and he is mild,
  He became a little child.
  I a child and thou a lamb,
  We are called by his name.
Little Lamb God bless thee.
Little Lamb God bless thee.

pp7–8, *Songs of Innocence and of Experience*

(Oxford University Press, 1990, [1789])

'The Sick Rose' (1794), William Blake

O rose thou art sick;
The invisible worm
That flies in the night,
In the howling storm,

Has found out thy bed
Of crimson joy,
And his dark secret love
Does thy life destroy.

p31, *Songs of Innocence and of Experience*

(Oxford University Press, 1990, [1794])

This extract is from halfway through Phase the First: 'The Maiden'. (The second is 'Maiden no More'.) Tess, a village farmworker aged 16, is visiting a wealthy family, whom her father believes are their long-lost relatives, for the first time. Alec is the swashbuckling son and heir to their country estate. By contrast, Tess is riddled with guilt because she has accidentally caused the death of her family's only asset, their horse, and is hoping to get a job with the new relatives, while her father has ambitions of marriage for her. Can you guess the sorry outcome of this episode, which occurs in a later chapter?

Extract 5
Tess of the d'Urbervilles (1891), Thomas Hardy
'Supposing we walk round the grounds to pass the time, my pretty Coz?'

Tess wished to abridge her visit as much as possible; but the young man was pressing, and she consented to accompany him. He conducted her about the lawns, and flower-beds, and conservatories; and thence to the fruit-garden and greenhouses, where he asked her if she liked strawberries.

'Yes,' said Tess, 'when they come.'

'They are already here.' D'Urberville began gathering specimens of the fruit for her, handing them back to her as he stooped; and, presently, selecting a specially fine product of the 'British Queen' variety, he stood up and held it by the stem to her mouth.

'No–no!' she said quickly, putting her fingers between his hand and her lips. 'I would rather take it in my own hand.'
'Nonsense!' he insisted; and in a slight distress she parted her lips and took it in.

They had spent some time wandering desultorily thus, Tess eating in a half-pleased, half-reluctant state whatever d'Urberville offered her. When she could consume no more of the strawberries he filled her little basket with them; and then the two passed round to the rose-trees, whence he gathered blossoms and gave her to put in her bosom. She obeyed like one in a dream, and when she could affix no more he himself tucked a bud or two into her hat, and heaped her basket with others in the prodigality of his bounty. At last, looking at his watch, he said, 'Now, by the time you have had something to eat, it will be time for you to leave, if you want to catch the carrier to Shaston. Come here, and I'll see what grub I can find.'

Stoke d'Urberville took her back to the lawn and into the tent, where he left her, soon reappearing with a basket of light luncheon, which he put before her himself. It was evidently the gentleman's wish not to be disturbed in this pleasant tête-à-tête by the servantry.

'Do you mind my smoking?' he asked.

'Oh, not at all, sir.'

He watched her pretty and unconscious munching through the skeins of smoke that pervaded the tent, and Tess Durbeyfield did not divine, as she innocently looked down at the roses in her bosom, that there behind the blue narcotic haze was potentially the 'tragic mischief' of her drama – one who stood fair to be the blood-red ray in the spectrum of her young life. She had an attribute which amounted to a disadvantage just now; and it was this that caused Alec d'Urberville's eyes to rivet themselves upon her. It was a luxuriance of aspect, a fulness of growth, which made her appear more of a woman than she really was. She had inherited the feature from her mother without the quality it denoted. It had troubled her mind occasionally, till her companions had said that it was a fault which time would cure.

She soon had finished her lunch. 'Now I am going home, sir,' she said, rising.

'And what do they call you?' he asked, as he accompanied her along the drive till they were out of sight of the house.

'Tess Durbeyfield, down at Marlott.'

'And you say your people have lost their horse?'

'I–killed him!' she answered, her eyes filling with tears as she gave particulars of Prince's death. 'And I don't know what to do for father on account of it!'

'I must think if I cannot do something. My mother must find a berth for you. But, Tess, no nonsense about 'd'Urberville';–'Durbeyfield' only, you know – quite another name.'

'I wish for no better, sir,' said she with something of dignity.

For a moment–only for a moment–when they were in the turning of the drive, between the tall rhododendrons and conifers, before the lodge became visible, he inclined his face towards her as if – but, no: he thought better of it, and let her go.

Thus the thing began. Had she perceived this meeting's import she might have asked why she was doomed to be seen and coveted that day by the wrong man, and not by some other man, the right and desired one in all respects–as nearly as humanity can supply the right and desired; yet to him who amongst her acquaintance might have approximated to this kind, she was but a transient impression, half forgotten.

In the ill-judged execution of the well-judged plan of things the call seldom produces the comer, the man to love rarely coincides with the hour for loving. Nature does not often say 'See!' to her poor creature at a time when seeing can lead to happy doing; or reply 'Here!' to a body's cry of 'Where?' till the hide-and-seek has become an irksome, outworn game. We may wonder whether at the acme and summit of the human progress these anachronisms will be corrected by a finer intuition, a closer interaction of the social machinery than that which now jolts us round and along; but such completeness is not to be prophesied, or even conceived as possible. Enough that in the present case, as in millions, it was not the two halves of a perfect whole that confronted each other at the perfect moment; a missing counterpart wandered independently about the earth waiting in cross obtuseness till the late time came. Out of which maladroit delay sprang anxieties, disappointments, shocks, catastrophes, and passing-strange destinies.

pp34–6 *Tess of the d'Urbervilles* (Wordsworth Classics, 2000 edn [1891])

Extract 6

'To His Coy Mistress' (c.1640s–1650s),
Andrew Marvell

Had we but world enough, and time,
This coyness, lady, were no crime.
We would sit down and think which way
To walk, and pass our long love's day;
Thou by the Indian Ganges' side
Shouldst rubies find; I by the tide
Of Humber would complain. I would
Love you ten years before the Flood;
And you should, if you please, refuse
Till the conversion of the Jews.
My vegetable love should grow
Vaster than empires, and more slow.
An hundred years should go to praise
Thine eyes, and on thy forehead gaze;
Two hundred to adore each breast,
But thirty thousand to the rest;
An age at least to every part,
And the last age should show your heart.
For, lady, you deserve this state,
Nor would I love at lower rate.

But at my back I always hear
Time's winged chariot hurrying near;
And yonder all before us lie
Deserts of vast eternity.

Thy beauty shall no more be found,
Nor, in thy marble vault, shall sound
My echoing song; then worms shall try
That long preserv'd virginity,
And your quaint honour turn to dust,
And into ashes all my lust.
The grave's a fine and private place,
But none I think do there embrace.

Now therefore, while the youthful hue
Sits on thy skin like morning dew,
And while thy willing soul transpires
At every pore with instant fires,
Now let us sport us while we may;
And now, like am'rous birds of prey,
Rather at once our time devour,
Than languish in his slow-chapp'd power.
Let us roll all our strength, and all
Our sweetness, up into one ball;
And tear our pleasures with rough strife
Thorough the iron gates of life.
Thus, though we cannot make our sun
Stand still, yet we will make him run.

pp250–52, *The Metaphysical Poets* (Penguin Classics, 1972 edn [c.1640s–1650s])

Extract 7

'Sonnet 116' (1609), William Shakespeare

Let me not to the marriage of true minds
Admit impediments; love is not love
Which alters when it alteration finds,
Or bends with the remover to remove.
O no, it is an ever-fixed mark,
That looks on tempests and is never shaken;
It is the star to every wand'ring bark,
Whose worth's unknown, although his height be taken.
Love's not Time's fool, though rosy lips and cheeks
Within his bending sickle's compass come;
Love alters not with his brief hours and weeks,
But bears it out even to the edge of doom.
If this be error and upon me proved,
I never writ, nor no man ever loved.

p343, *Shakespeare's Sonnets* (Arden, 1997 edn [1609])

Extract 8

'Funeral Blues' (1938), W.H. Auden

Stop all the clocks, cut off the telephone,
Prevent the dog from barking with a juicy bone,
Silence the pianos and with muffled drum
Bring out the coffin, let the mourners come.

Let aeroplanes circle moaning overhead
Scribbling on the sky the message He Is Dead,
Put crepe bows round the white necks of the public doves,
Let the traffic policemen wear black cotton gloves.

He was my North, my South, my East and West,
My working week and my Sunday rest,
My noon, my midnight, my talk, my song;
I thought that love would last forever: I was wrong.

The stars are not wanted now; put out every one,
Pack up the moon and dismantle the sun,
Pour away the ocean and sweep up the wood;
For nothing now can ever come to any good.

p21, *W. H. Auden: Poems selected by John Fuller* (Faber, 2000 edn [1938])

Set in southern India in the 1960s–1990s, the cover of this novel says that it explores the tragic fate of a family which 'tampered with the laws that lay down who should be loved, and how'. Velutha, a Paravan man, an Untouchable, has broken the caste law by having a sexual relationship with Ammu (Margaret), a Christian caste woman, a Touchable, when she was forbidden even to touch him or to walk across a floor in his footsteps. This extract is from the final chapter, 'The Cost of Living'. It poignantly recalls Velutha's relationship with Ammu and his part in *The God of Small Things*.

Extract 9
The God of Small Things (1997), Arundhati Roy

Even later, on the thirteen nights that followed this one, instinctively they stuck to the Small Things. The Big Things ever lurked inside. They knew that there was nowhere for them to go. They had nothing. No future. So they stuck to the small things.

They laughed at ant-bites on each other's bottoms. At clumsy caterpillars sliding off the ends of leaves, at overturned beetles that couldn't right themselves. At the pair of small fish that always sought Velutha out in the river and bit him. At a particularly devout praying mantis. At the minute spider who lived in a crack in the wall of the black verandah of the History House and camouflaged himself by covering his body with bits of rubbish – a sliver of wasp wing. Part of a cobweb. Dust. Leaf rot. The empty thorax of a dead bee. *Chappu Thamburan*, Velutha called him. Lord Rubbish. One night they contributed to his wardrobe – a flake of garlic skin – and were deeply offended when he rejected it along with the rest of his armour from which he emerged – disgruntled, naked, snot-coloured. As though he deplored their taste in clothes. For a few days he remained in this suicidal state of disdainful undress. The rejected shell of garbage stayed standing, like an outmoded world-view. An antiquated philosophy. Then it crumbled. Gradually *Chappu Thamburan* acquired a new ensemble.

Without admitting it to each other or themselves, they linked their fates, their futures (their Love, their Madness, their Hope, their Infinnate Joy) to his. They checked on him every night (with growing panic as time went by) to see if he had survived the day. They fretted over his frailty. His smallness. The adequacy of his camouflage. His seemingly self-destructive pride. They grew to love his eclectic taste. His shambling dignity.

They chose him because they knew that they had to put their faith in fragility. Stick to Smallness. Each time they parted, they extracted only one small promise from each other.

'*Tomorrow*?'

'*Tomorrow.*'

They knew that things could change in a day. They were right about that.

They were wrong about *Chappu Thamburan*, though. He outlived Velutha. He fathered future generations. He died of natural causes.

That first night, on the day that Sophie Mol came, Velutha watched his lover dress. When she was ready she squatted facing him. She touched him lightly with her fingers and left a trail of goosebumps on his skin. Like flat chalk on a blackboard. Like breeze in a paddyfield. Like jet-streaks in a blue church sky. He took her face in his hands and drew it towards his. He closed his eyes and smelled her skin. Ammu laughed.

Yes, Margaret, she thought. *We do it to each other.*

She kissed his closed eyes and stood up. Velutha with his back against the mangosteen tree watched her walk away.

She had a dry rose in her hair.

She turned to say it once again: '*Naaley*.'
Tomorrow.

pp338–40, *The God of Small Things* (Harper Perennial, 2004 edn [1997])

Extract 10 comes from Tony Kushner's drama about AIDS, identity in crisis and the fears of an impending millennium. Here, near the end of the play, Harper, the valium-addicted and unfulfilled agoraphobic wife of a court clerk, has temporarily left her ordinary reality and gone to Antarctica with Mr Lies, her imaginary friend who is a travel agent.

Extract 10

Angels in America (1992), Tony Kushner
HARPER *in a very white, cold place, with a brilliant blue sky above; a delicate snowfall. She is dressed, for warmth, in layers upon layers of mismatched clothing. The sound of the sea, faint.*

HARPER. Snow! Ice! Mountains of ice! Where am I? I…

I feel better, I do, I…feel better. There are ice crystals in my lungs, wonderful and sharp. And the snow smells like cold, crushed peaches. And there's something…some current of blood in the wind, how strange, it has that iron taste.

MR LIES. Ozone.

HARPER. Ozone! Wow! Where am I?

MR LIES. The Kingdom of Ice, the bottom-most part of the world.

HARPER. (*looking around, then realising*) Antarctica. This is Antarctica!

MR LIES. Cold shelter for the shattered. No sorrow here, tears freeze.

HARPER. Antarctica, Antarctica, oh boy oh boy, LOOK at this, I…Wow, I must've really snapped the tether, huh?

MR LIES. Apparently…

HARPER. That's great. I want to stay here forever. Set up camp. Build things. Build a city, an enormous city made up of frontier forts, dark wood and green roofs and high gates made of pointed logs and bonfires burning on every street corner. I should build by a river. Where are the forests?

MR LIES. No timber here. Too cold. Ice, no trees.

HARPER. Oh details! I'm sick of details! I'll plant them and grow them. I'll live off caribou fat. I'll melt it over the bonfires and drink it from long, curved goat-horn cups. It'll be great. I want to make a new world here. So that I never have to go home again.

MR LIES. As long as it lasts. Ice has a way of melting…

HARPER. No. Forever. I can have anything I want here – maybe even companionship, someone who has…desire for me. You, maybe.

MR LIES. It's against the by-laws of the International Order of the Travel Agents to get involved with clients. Rules are rules. Anyway, I'm not the one you really want.

HARPER. There isn't anyone…maybe an Eskimo. Who could ice-fish for food. And help me build a nest for when the baby comes.

MR LIES. There are no Eskimos in Antarctica. And you're not really pregnant. You made that up.

HARPER. Well all of this is made up. So if the snow feels cold I'm pregnant. Right? Here, I can be pregnant. And I can have any kind of a baby I want.

MR LIES. This is a retreat, a vacuum, its virtue is that it lacks everything; deep-freeze for feelings. You can be numb and safe here, that's what you came for. Respect the delicate ecology of your illusions.

HARPER. You mean like no Eskimo in Antarctica.

MR LIES. Correcto. Ice and snow, no Eskimo. Even hallucinations have laws.

HARPER. Well then who's that?
The ESKIMO *appears.*
MR LIES. An Eskimo.
HARPER. An Antarctic Eskimo. A fisher of the polar deep.
MR LIES. There's something wrong with this picture.
The ESKIMO *beckons.*

HARPER. I'm going to like this place. It's my own National Geographic Special! Oh! Oh! (*She holds her stomach.*) I think…I think I felt her kicking. Maybe I'll give birth to a baby covered with thick white fur, and that way she won't be cold. My breasts will be full of hot cocoa so she doesn't get chilly. And if it gets really cold, she'll have a pouch I can crawl into. Like a marsupial. We'll mend together. That's what we'll do; we'll mend.

pp77–9, Act 3, Scene 4, *Angels in America* (Nick Hern Books, 1992)

Summary

This chapter has introduced you to comparing texts from different periods across different genres. You have explored how to do a comparative analysis of cross-period, cross-genre texts, and considered how to:

- find similarities and differences
- approach examination questions
- analyse a range of extracts.

Examination or coursework

The first factor you need to consider when you compare texts is how you will be assessed, either by examination or by coursework.

Examination

If you are comparing texts for analysis in examination conditions, you need to prepare for the following two eventualities:

1. The focus of the comparison is already chosen for you and is set out in the topic key words of the question/s.
2. The time allowed will determine how much of that given focus you can reasonably compare.

Set questions

As you will not know the focus of your examination questions prior to the exam, you need to ensure that you are prepared for anything that might be included. You can do this by practising responses to the several different ways in which your texts can be compared. On top of your knowledge and understanding of the texts, you need to grasp the ways in which they connect and/or differ. Use the Assessment Objectives tested in your examination as a guide to what you can compare. This preparation will help you to be ready to select appropriate aspects of the texts to compare in response to a given task or question. Knowledge of your texts is only a starting point. Answering the question is the key. Comparing texts means that the comparison is the key to unlocking relevant content for your answer.

Time limits

Plan an answer that you can complete and review in the allotted time. Do not try to write everything you know about your texts. Knowing more about a group of texts does not mean that you can always compare more. Select a few key points that will allow you to create some important or interesting comparisons that the question opens up to you. Once you have planned your response, you need a structure that can be followed in the time you have. Your structure should allow you to conclude your comparative analysis before the end of your plan if you run out of time. Chapter 10 suggests ways of 'balancing your response' to make sure that your comparative coverage does not suffer too much if you do find that time becomes an issue for you in the examination. The pitfall of time mismanagement is that your overall marks will be heavily affected. Once you go over the time limit for a question, you are using time from another question.

Preparing for the examination

Before the examination, practise how much you can meaningfully compare in the time allowed by answering questions on past papers, teacher-set tasks and ones you devise yourself or with other students. It is likely that the subject matter (AO1) will be tested, so prepare to make connections across the presentation of characters, themes and messages. It is likely that the writer's choice of techniques (AO2) will be assessed, so look for the key words that ask you to do that: for example, 'ways in which', 'presents', 'dramatic importance'. If critical response (AO3) is assessed, you are likely to compare how your texts can be interpreted in the light of a view that the question states. Keep the focus on comparing how the view is relevant to each text. If context (AO4) is assessed, you are likely to analyse the effect of some shared contexts, either of period and/or styles and subgenres. Check exactly what is being assessed before you start your comparative preparation before the examination.

Coursework

A comparative analysis by coursework has three main differences from an analysis by examination:

1. You have more control of the task and what you are going to compare about your texts.
2. You have more time to explore and research the ways in which you compare your texts.
3. You have opportunities to revisit and redraft the ways in which you have made your comparisons.

Remember that coursework is not the easy option. It demands discipline as much as it offers freedom.

Control of the task

Whether you or your teacher has set the task, you need to make sure that the focus of your comparison is a reasonable task for the word count you have to meet. If your response is too short, you are unlikely to reach your potential. If it is too long, you might lose some tightness in your focus. Either way, this could affect your final marks. Some examination boards penalise if you do not meet the word count, by deducting marks for straying too far from what they have asked. All examination boards agree that you penalise yourself if you go too far under or over the word count, as this means that the focus of the task is not met. That can affect the marks awarded. Your title and ideas need to be rigorously checked to make sure they are feasible for the number of words you have. Your plan needs to account for how you will use your words to make your comparisons. Usually, when coursework runs out of steam halfway through, it is because the candidate has plenty to say about their texts, but not very much to compare.

Time to explore and research

This is the jewel in the coursework crown and you should take what is offered. You have more time, as well as control, to polish your work and avoid nervous errors that you cannot go back and correct in an examination. As a result, you need to put even more effort and thought into your response to coursework than into your responses to examination questions. It is expected that the first draft is the best you can do within the conditions under which it is set. Use the second-draft stage for any further teaching and learning you need on how to *edit* your work, so that you focus the argument and meet the word limits. The skill of editing will then stand you in equally good stead in examinations.

The comparison should be something that interests you and develops your comparative understanding in ways that an examination cannot. An examination-style question is often a poor model for your essay title. The task should give you scope to find out something new about how and why it is interesting to link your texts. It should be tailored to get the best out of you, your texts, the time and resources you have available.

'Explore' is the key word in coursework. You have time to follow a few routes at the planning and research stages and see where your comparisons take you. If they prove fruitless or dry up, look at how your original idea can be altered to get to a comparison you are happy with. By the time you write a first draft, you should have a clear basis for a comparison of aspects of your texts that have caught your imagination at some point in your study. Use the defining features of coursework – control and time – to make a comparison that you enjoy and care about. You do not have this opportunity in the examination, so use it here, where you can.

Comparative analysis is a high-order skill, and completing such a task is impressive: to teachers, examiners, universities and employers. It shows that you can select what matters, investigate relationships, make decisions based on your findings, and tie it all together by following a line of argument that you set up and conclude. You should be impressed with yourself after that, whatever grade you get. The coursework is where you can really learn how to do this. It assesses comparative analysis in a different way from an examination. An examination tests whether you can respond to someone else's agenda and apply your comparative knowledge and understanding of texts to a task that you do not choose or control.

Coursework encourages:

- a thoughtful, considered weighing-up of facts and possibilities
- several ways of seeing and looking around a problem until you find a way through the mass of information
- grasping the connections you need to reach a conclusion.

Your coursework comparative analysis is based on a critical reading of a range of evidence and helps to develop a life skill that you can refine wherever you go. Make a good job of your comparative coursework; you will not regret it.

Revisiting and redrafting

If you have read and taken the advice in the paragraphs above, your first draft will already be nearly as good as you can achieve. Your first draft should be a complete work in itself, but one that can be improved in the ways you select, organise and refine your material. The comparative analysis should be clear by this stage. Your teacher is not there to tell you what you must compare, or how or why you must compare your texts. They are there to suggest how you can edit and polish your analysis. If you have made the appropriate effort throughout the task, trying to improve a comparison by revisiting it time and again is not always a good use of your time. If you have not made the effort earlier, last-minute attempts are usually of limited benefit. Either way, the first draft is by far the most substantial task. Redrafting is necessary, but should be secondary to the comparisons you have already made and the line of argument you have already agreed.

Access to your texts

How you approach comparative analysis can depend on how much access you have to your texts in the examination.

Closed-text examinations

A closed-text examination is one where you are not permitted to take your texts into the examination. This method of assessment means that you can expect a particular style of question. For example, you cannot be expected to recall and respond in detail to the language of specific extracts named in a closed-book examination. The questions are likely to let you select evidence from somewhere in the text that you think is appropriate for your comparison and line of argument. Because the text is not in front of you, the kind of evidence you provide can be different from when you do have the text in front of you. These factors affect a comparative analysis because the focus needs to be on what is reasonable for you to remember without the texts as a prompt. In closed-text exams, the examiner will not expect exact quotation, especially from prose and drama texts. He or she will be looking for apt and relevant references to the text to support the points you make.

Look at the kinds of question you are asked to answer if you are preparing for a closed-book examination. Identify the Assessment Objectives you need to address. If AO2 (how writers use language, form and structure) is assessed, work out how you can compare this without access to the texts. Ask yourself the following questions: How will comparison of the structures (narrative, dramatic, poetic) be relevant? How can I explore the importance of form and genre? Form and genre features are always easier ways to address texts in a closed-book exam, especially in prose and drama texts, because you can look at bigger patterns that are easier to remember than the details of word use. Which features of language are likely to be comparable? Are they the dominant features of the language used in your texts? How will you compare what is significant about their effects in the text?

Open-book examinations

If you have an open-book examination then it is a requirement that you take your texts into the examination. It is not considered to be optional, as some kind of a bonus. The requirement means that the questions will be written in ways that demand that you consult your texts. Typical questions of this assessment method require your detailed response to specific aspects of a named extract. If you have some access to your texts, check how central the writers' techniques are to your comparative analysis. AO2 may be dominant, or at least equal, to the other Assessment Objectives you must consider if you have access to the texts.

Printed extracts

Printed extracts of any of your comparative texts are a feature of some examinations. Printed extracts are a sort of halfway-house between open- and closed-book examinations. If you take an examination which uses printed extracts, check how you must use them in your comparison. Are they the focus of a detailed comparison? Is that focus named in the question or are you expected to select the focus yourself from the printed extract/s? Are they a prompt for aspects of the text you must compare beyond the extract, in other parts of the texts you study? Is there a printed extract of one that you have to compare with ones that do not appear on the paper? Is the printed extract used as a 'trigger' text that you might not have studied at all? Once you know how the printed extract is used, you can identify links between the printed extract/s and what is required from your comparison. This is likely to include shared subject matter or/and context.

Some examination boards refer to printed extracts as 'source booklets'. This is when the extract comes from a wider anthology that you have already studied. The extract can come from anywhere in the anthology, so it is not seen as completely prepared in the way that a set text is seen.

Some examination boards use pre-release material, issued a week before the examination. This is where you get a package of extracts that you have not previously studied, from texts that are not set for the examination. This approach gives you time to familiarise yourself with the materials before you see the questions set on the extracts in the examination.

Unseen extracts

Some examinations feature an unseen extract. The previous section on 'printed extracts' asked you to consider whether it is one that you might not have studied or prepared at all. Even if you find an 'unseen' extract on the exam paper which is very familiar to you, it is important to re-read it very carefully in the light of the question. Regurgitating a response you have covered in class, without examining the context or group of texts in which it has been put, might not be appropriate or relevant to the question.

An unseen extract requires you to adopt specific approaches in your comparison. Are you comparing more than one unseen extract? Are they from the same or different genres? Are they from the same or different periods? Do you need to compare the importance of any shared contexts? If you only address one unseen extract within your comparison, also ask these questions of the texts you have studied, in comparison with each other and the unseen. If you have to compare it with texts that you have already prepared, what is the unseen extract bringing to your analysis? Why has it been selected for you? If the question includes an unseen extract, remember how the Assessment Objectives are applied to your comparative analysis. Check how important it is for you to compare aspects of style – language, form, structure, subgenre – between the texts you have been given and the ones you already know. Unless the extracts are complete texts, such as short poems, it is much harder to compare form and structure in unseen extracts, as you do not always know how the extract is situated within the whole text. Check how important and helpful it is to consider the shared contexts and/ or subject matter.

The advantage of the unseen extract is that you can bring your own, unlearned response to a text you do not know. Many examiners believe that this is a true test of how well you have developed the skill of literary analysis and critical reading. You cannot offload anyone else's opinions and ideas in a relevant response to an unseen extract. Unseen analysis represents what you really think, know and can do alone when faced with a literary text. Use this to your advantage and do not be afraid to express your considered personal response. Make meaning from what you see in front of you and how it connects with the texts you already know.

9   Text-based issues

Whole texts or extracts

Your comparative analysis requires you to compare either whole texts and/ or extracts. Let us look at ways of working with these different experiences of the texts.

Whole texts

If you are comparing whole texts, either for examination or coursework, you are not expected to compare everything about each of them in your response. That is impossible and can lead to a generalised approach that is of little use to your comparative analysis. The examination question or coursework task often directs your comparison. It could be a specific part of each text – for example, particular episode/s, specific feature/s such as the effects of the setting, mood, voice or structure, or the presentation of subject matter such as named character/s or theme/s. Some examination questions might be less specific, and ask you to compare how your texts all belong to the shared context. Here you have more freedom, but also more responsibility, to select the links that connect your whole texts.

When you compare whole texts:

- you have an overview of the texts, which increases your overall knowledge and understanding of what each writer is trying to do across the entire text
- you can select your evidence from anywhere in the texts that supports your argument and fulfils the comparisons you are trying to make.

Extracts

When you compare extracts, you need to be aware that they can be analysed on two levels. You can approach them as individual pieces of writing and also as part of a 'bigger picture', if they come from a collection or a larger piece of prose or drama that you have studied.

Sometimes the examination paper provides you with extracts to analyse as part of your comparison. This might include one or more unseen extracts or printed extracts that come from set texts you have already studied. Sometimes you provide the extracts for your answer. As part of your examination preparation, analysis of an anthology, pre-release materials and wider reading encourage you to compare extracts from whole texts as well as those which are complete, short texts.

When you compare extracts:

- you are being encouraged to explore a specific aspect of a text, such as its language use, narrative voice or how it is influenced by a shared context
- the key is in the detail. The comparisons you make should be focused on specific references to lines within the extract, whichever Assessment Objectives you address.

Comparison of extracts requires you to pay particular attention to the language, even if you do not have the extract in front of you, as that forms the basis of what you know about each short piece.

Connect the extracts through what they show you from their language, tone, mood and subject matter. Look at how the shared context/s connect them in any wider sense that you have studied or know about. Compare how aspects of the extract structure could be setting up the plot. Look at how the voice presents a particular viewpoint that is important elsewhere in the texts. Compare ways in which any introductions to character/s and their relationships foreshadow, conclude and/or contradict what you know about the characters from other parts of the texts. If you have enough evidence, compare how the ideas, messages and themes of the whole texts are reflected in the extract.

10 Balancing your response

Balancing your response is about juggling not only multiple texts, but also multiple approaches to reading and studying your texts. Comparing two or more texts by giving them equal attention is a typical way to make connections for your analysis. This approach has been covered throughout the book.

Wider reading

In addition to the named whole texts that are set for your examination and coursework, some examination boards require you to do some wider reading of additional texts or extracts as a part of your overall study. Wider reading can be set by the teacher, sometimes as a group activity, sometimes outside of classwork. You might also be encouraged to choose your own wider reading by investigating texts or extracts yourself that can help you with the main texts and ideas that you are studying.

How wider reading is comparative

AO3 makes clear that an essential part of literary study is 'exploring connections and comparisons between literary texts'. Wider reading is usually used to make comparisons with the other reading you are doing. This could be the wider reading you bring to an examination, to compare with either a whole text that you have studied and prepared in detail or with an unseen extract that you first encounter on an examination paper. Some examination boards give specific instructions about the range of wider reading you must bring to your answer – for example, a reference to each genre of poetry, prose and drama. Others ask you to decide what is most relevant to your answer. Either way, the point of wider reading is that you 'read around' the area of literature you are mainly studying. You can learn more about how your central texts work by reading other texts that connect with them. This is especially true where there is a shared context of period and/or style. The advantage of wider reading is that you are encouraged to choose from any number of other texts or extracts. As a result, your wider reading can reveal something that you find particularly interesting or enjoyable that illuminates your main texts.

Using wider reading

Balancing wider reading in your comparative analysis is not a matter of proportion or percentage. There are no rules and regulations that tell you exactly how much evidence of wider reading must be in your answer. Usually, examination boards will give instructions or guidance on question papers that show you how to prioritise if there are texts you must focus on. When examination boards do not publish that information, they are letting you decide. Overall, they are most interested in the use you make of your wider reading, rather than the quantity of reading you demonstrate.

The way in which you can use your wider reading is to show something particular about the main focus of your study.

> **Links**
>
> For more information on Comparing 'All three genres', see Chapter 6, pages 72–76.

Comparing wider reading with whole texts

If your main focus is a named whole text, the references to wider reading should connect specifically to the points you make about the main text. For example, you could analyse a Shakespearean sonnet and refer to a sonnet from a different period:

- to compare subject matter (AO1), perhaps a debate on romantic love
- to compare how the structure of the sonnet lays out the argument (AO2), perhaps on the development of jealousy
- to compare how the sonnet structure changes over time (AO4), perhaps to explore different social responses to romantic love.

The similarities between your wider reading and the main text can also show you how the Shakespearean sonnet belongs to a literary, poetic, tradition that has some connections with sonnets from other periods. This is only one example. Your connections between a main text and wider reading are likely to include ways in which form, structure, themes and ideas are used to deliver the writers' messages across time.

Wider reading that illuminates a whole text can be from any period or genre, but there will need to be some clear and overall connection that you can draw from subject matter, technique and/or context.

Comparing wider reading with unseen extracts

If your main focus is an unseen extract, the references to wider reading should still connect specifically to the points you make about the main text. The unseen extract can be used as a 'trigger' to explore the connections between your wider reading extracts and texts. Your chosen references should all have some similarities with the unseen. Use the unseen extract as a starting point to compare features of subject matter, technique and/ or context that explore connections with your wider reading. The process will reveal some differences for you to analyse. Your conclusion could then weigh up why these references belong together in your response.

Be clear about the focus of the question and your understanding of the relationship between any main text(s) or extracts and your wider reading. Develop an analysis that helps you to make substantial connections between the texts in your answer, based on the guidance above.

Core and partner texts

Some examination boards approach comparison through the study of core and partner texts. The core text is the main text which must be studied throughout in detail. The partner text is one that is studied in less detail. The purpose of this approach is to show the reader how the two connect, and how the partner text shows you something about the core text. This is not to say that one is more important than the other – either within literary study in general or in your own studies. It is more about approaches and how the partner text is being used. It is there to support your explorations of the main text. You are likely to focus on the main text in your task and use the partner text as an extension or support for your main argument. You will be expected to plan and write a response that shows how the core text explores the ideas, techniques and/or contexts in the question. For each point you make, decide if the partner text can be used to support your analysis. If it can, extend your point to refer to the partner text. If it cannot, move to your next point about the core text. You are more concerned with similarities in this approach to comparative analysis and are likely to pay less attention to the differences you might find. This is because you are not expected to produce an analysis which gives equal weight to the core and partner texts.

Meeting the Assessment Objectives

You have been considering ways to meet the Assessment Objectives as part of your comparative analysis. Our focus has been on the comparative element and how the other Assessment Objectives make up the remaining elements of your response:

AO1

You always need something to compare. Subject matter is a part of every comparison because you are comparing what the texts are about: for example, themes, characterisation and ideas.

AO2

You can be asked to compare how the subject matter is presented: the writers' techniques of form, structure and language.

AO3

You can be asked to compare texts in the light of a view or interpretation: your own and/or someone else's, such as a critic or a recognised critical opinion.

AO4

You can be asked to compare your texts within context: a shared typicality, such as period and/or genre and/or subgenre. This could be a named context or a range of contexts.

Balancing AOs in your answer

The more Assessment Objectives you have to address, the more complex your comparative analysis becomes. Balancing your response to Assessment Objectives as part of a comparative analysis of your texts becomes vital. The approaches and activities in this book have steered you to balance your response across Assessment Objectives. To put this into practice, always examine the types of question or task you will need to undertake in examinations and coursework. Identify the focus of the question; examine the key words and the importance of each key word or part of the question. Plan an answer that shows how you will address each part of the question and its importance.

Do not write an answer that 'ticks off' Assessment Objectives as if they are the focus of the question itself. The focus of the question will be some aspect of subject matter and/or technique and/or context, perhaps also interpreted through a particular view. Your comparative analysis is likely to incorporate points that address several Assessment Objectives. For example, you might compare how subject matter is presented, which leads you directly into techniques. You might compare how the subject matter or specific techniques are typical of a subgenre (style) or era (period), which leads you directly into contexts. You might argue that the presentation of subject matter can be interpreted in a range of ways, which leads you directly into a critical response.

Balancing your response to meet Assessment Objectives can be done from within your argument in this way. Your comparative analysis includes your response to what else is being assessed, so that it is all part of one answer.

Structuring a comparative analysis

The best way to structure a comparative analysis is to work through the connections that your texts reveal, connection by connection.

Connection by connection

Approaching your texts connection by connection enables you to answer the question most effectively. This is the most rigorous way to compare your texts. If you respond to the task by addressing a range of comparisons, then you automatically attempt a comparative analysis. Examine the question and consider your texts and/or extracts. Plan an answer that addresses the main focus of the question by covering the key words. Select a range of ways, with evidence, that compare how your texts explore or reflect the focus of the question. Look at how each text or extract does this across the points that you want to make. You will need to adjust your answer to respond to particular requirements of your comparative study – for example, comparing more than two texts, using wider reading or core and partner texts, balancing your response to the Assessment Objectives in your answer.

Begin by identifying the subject matter, use of techniques and the significance of contexts in each of the texts or extracts you are going to compare. Identify a shared aspect of the three texts that you expect to find or know is there from your previous knowledge and understanding of the texts or type of texts. This might be a theme, or the role of a specific character, or a setting or structure, and the ways in which the technique is used. Work methodically with your chosen feature across each text. Compare similarities and differences between how it is presented and how it is significant, in either the extract and/or the whole text. This works particularly well with texts that have a shared context that you have studied. The context might be a shared period, social concern or literary subgenre. Be careful to avoid any assertion, generalisation or comparison which either lacks evidence or tries to fit evidence to the shared context. Just because you know that the texts share some aspects of typicality does not mean that your examples will conform to that, so always base your arguments on direct evidence from the text.

Further reading

General works

The *Cambridge Contexts in Literature* series is an excellent series targeted at A Level students in key areas of study such as:

Adrian Barlow, *The Great War in British Literature*, (Cambridge University Press, 2000).

Peter Buckroyd and Jane Ogborn, *Satire* (Cambridge University Press, 2001).

Barbara Dennis, *The Victorian Novel* (Cambridge University Press, 2000).

David Stevens, *The Gothic Tradition* (Cambridge University Press, 2000).

Mary Ward, *The Literature of Love* (Cambridge University Press, 2009).

Adrian Beard, *The Language of Literature* (Routledge, 2003). A very useful guide to how analysis of technique provides a basis for comparisons in context.

Richard Gill, *Mastering English Literature* (Palgrave Macmillan, third edition, 2006). A definitive and excellent guide to analysing literature in all its aspects, genres, periods, contexts and techniques. It is part of the excellent Palgrave *Master Series* and is also recommended by the WJEC as secondary reading for A Level English Literature students.

Carol Leach, *Elizabethan and Jacobean Drama 1590–1640 in Context* (Nelson Thornes, 2013). A useful and current guide for comparing groups of same genre, same period texts.

Carol Leach, *Post-1990 Texts in Context* (Nelson Thornes, 2013). A useful and current guide for comparing groups of different genre, same period texts.

Nicola Onyett, *Comparing Texts* (Routledge, 2005). A useful guide to comparing a range of literary texts across genre and period with some supporting non-fictional and critical extracts to enrich the connections.

AQA (A)

Stella Canwell, *Literature of World War One* (Nelson Thornes, 2008).

Stella Canwell and Jane Ogborn, *AQA English Literature A A2* (Nelson Thornes, 2008). A comprehensive and excellent coverage of comparative approaches to 'Love throughout the Ages' and the coursework extended essay: cross-genre, cross-period including Shakespeare.

Carol Leach, *The Struggle for Identity in Modern Literature* (Nelson Thornes, 2008).

Ian Stewart, *Victorian Literature*, (Nelson Thornes, 2008).

AQA (B)

Adrian Beard and Peter Bunten, *AQA English Literature B A2* (Nelson Thornes, 2008).

Adrian Beard and Alan Kent, *AQA English Literature B AS* (Nelson Thornes, Second Edition, 2012).

OCR

Various, *Comparative Essays for OCR A2 English Literature* (Oxford University Press, 2013). Current and tailored critical essays based on the set drama and poetry texts. Endorsed by OCR. Written for A2 students by seven senior examiners, including Catherine Thompson and David Johnson.

Various, *Critical Anthology for OCR AS English Literature* (Oxford University Press, 2008).

Edexcel

Barbara Bleiman, Sue Dymoke, Ian McMechan, Mike Royston and Jennifer Smith, *Edexcel AS English Literature* (Pearson, 2008).

Mike Royston and Jackie Moore, *Edexcel A2 English Literature* (Pearson, 2009).

Glossary

accent the way words are pronounced according to geographical setting or social class.

analysis a structured examination of aspects of your text supported by evidence and your own commentary.

B

ballad a song that tells a story, originally set to music, with basic rhythms to make it easy to remember and to sing.

C

chronological narrative one that moves forward in time.

cliché an overused phrase or opinion based on a metaphor or simile that makes it seem like empty or meaningless language.

colloquial language/ colloquialisms informal, casual, conversational words and phrases; language that you might speak yourself.

comedy a form of drama with a happy or satisfying outcome for the plot and its main characters.

comic relief a comic or funny episode in a tragedy play that lessens the effects or reflects the ideas of the main tragic plot.

comparative cross-reference of texts to see the ways in which they are similar and different.

connections links or common ground between different texts or aspects of text.

contemporary something happening within its own time. This can be in the past or the present. For example, First World War contemporary matters are those happening in that period. Today's contemporary issues are those happening now, at this moment.

context a range of factors affecting how texts are written, received and understood.

core texts whole texts which you study in detail, supported by a partner text.

critical discussion analysis that weighs up the ideas in the question, according to different interpretations (yours and/or other readers or critics) of the text.

D

dialect the language variety of a geographical setting or social class.

dramatic monologue has two aspects worth remembering:
1. It is a piece in which a single speaker addresses an imaginary audience.
2. It has links with lyric poems.

dynamic something which changes, develops or moves.

dystopia a fictional place or society, including imaginary settings, which is damaged, frightening or has stopped functioning.

E

elegy a poem of serious reflection, usually a lament for the dead.

English Renaissance a time of great thirst for new knowledge which produced significant developments in drama and the arts, as well as science, religion, law, navigation and travel.

epistolary novel where the novel is written as a series of letters to carry the chronological narrative.

existentialism a philosophical theory based on the existence of the individual as a free and responsible agent determining his or her own development. A central idea is that God is dead and that life has no other meaning than what we give it.

F

flashback narrative one that initially looks back in time from the present to a moment in the past, then moves forwards again, towards the present moment.

free verse poetry written without the rules of rhyme, stanza pattern or metre, with no predetermined form so any new shape is possible

G

genre a specific type of text. In literature there are three: drama, poetry and prose.

H

history a form of drama that focuses on historical events which often acted as military or royal propaganda or criticism.

hybrid a product whose style has blended two or more styles into a new product.

I

ideology political, social and cultural beliefs and ideas.

interior monologue like stream of consciousness but spoken (rather than just thought or written) by the character and directed at the audience.

intertextuality 1. When a text responds to ideas, language or direct references adopted or adapted from an earlier text.
2. Where a writer refers to another person's work or textual innovations within his or her own text.

irony using language to mean the opposite of the normal meaning of the word, phrase, idea.

K

kitchen-sink realism drama which presents domestic hardships of ordinary people in realistic settings.

M

macro the overview or 'big picture': these contexts are concerned with the world outside of the text – historical and political, social and cultural.

magic realism a movement which blends the styles of a fairy tale or mythical fantasy and harsh social reality. Both plays and novels use this style.

message(s)   opinions, ideas and conclusions that the writer communicates through the text.

metaphysical   intellectual poetry, usually from 17th-century England. More interested in analysing feelings than expressing them.

N

narrative poem   has two aspects worth remembering:
1. It is designed as a story with a plot and characters.
2. It was the main narrative form before the novel was born.

naturalistic   natural-sounding language, as it would actually be spoken, aloud or in someone's head.

9/11   The name given to the destruction of the World Trade Center, or Twin Towers, in New York on 11 September 2001, with two hijacked planes.

P

parody   an imitation of the style of a particular writer, artist, genre, subgenre, voice or individual with deliberate exaggeration for comic effect.

partner texts   whole texts which you study to help you understand your more detailed study of core texts.

period   a particular time or era in history.

protagonist   a central character, whose fortunes in the plot are important throughout the play.

pun   a form of wordplay, where a word is given two or more separate and unconnected meanings.

R

realisable text   one which can be brought to life with actors, the drama genre.

realism   the presentation of characters, language, setting and plots which reflects the experiences and behaviour of ordinary people and everyday life.

reception   how we experience, understand and receive ideas, products and events.

resolution   the dramatic outcome in which all aspects of the plot, structure, themes and character relationships are concluded.

Restoration comedy   style of drama that flourished in London after the Restoration of the monarchy with Charles II in 1660.

Revenge tragedy   a tragedy play that focuses on the motive, planning and execution of death by revenge, usually involving multiple deaths.

S

satire   ironic comedy which mocks and judges people, groups or organisations and their vices, such as corruption or greed.

sonnet   14 lines of iambic pentameter verse. Different types of sonnet follow particular rhyme schemes.

split narrative   one that has at least two narrative strands running in any direction through time.

stream of consciousness naturalistic language providing an uninterrupted 'stream' of the characters' thoughts and feelings.

stylised   a style that is artificial rather than realistic.

subgenre   a division within a genre, such as science fiction or tragedy.

subject matter   what the text is about: its plot, themes and ideas.

suspension of disbelief   accepting the reality that you are shown in a play or a film, regardless of whether you would believe it outside of that context.

sympathy   emotional identification with a character's situation.

T

Theatre of the Absurd   drama in which normal conventions and dramatic structure are ignored or changed, in order to present life as futile and human behaviour as irrational.

tone   the attitude of the writer to the text itself: for example, formal, playful, sarcastic.

tragedy   a form of drama concerned with human suffering and multiple deaths, traditionally caused partly by the flaws of the tragic hero(ine).

tragic hero(ine)   a flawed hero(ine) who makes mistakes and causes the downfall of several characters, along with him- or herself.

tragi-comedy   a play with tragic beginnings that ends in comedy.

typicality   where several texts share common or similar contexts, especially within the same period.

U

unseen   a text or extract used in some examination questions, but not set for classroom study or preparation.

W

war on terror   the ongoing military actions of the UK and the US, and initially other European countries, to stamp out Al Qaeda and protect the UK, the US and Europe from terror threats and actions.

Western literary canon   a body of literature throughout history and across genres that the Western academic establishment considers as classics for all time and core texts for study.

wider reading   your reading of texts that helps you to understand your set texts and/or an overall shared theme and context.

Index

Acknowledgements

The author and the publisher would also like to thank the following for permission to reproduce material:

p9-10, 83–84, AQA examination questions reproduced by permission of AQA Education (AQA); p9, 83–84, OCR – A2 GCE English Literature – (F663) Drama and Poetry pre-1800. Published 2012; p10, examination question reproduced by kind permission of WJEC; p10, 83–84, Pearson Education Ltd (Edexcel); p24, copyright Siegfried Sassoon by kind permission of the Estate of George Sassoon; pp26–27, Sheenagh Pugh, 'Intercity Lullaby' from *Selected Poems* (Bridgend, Seren, 1990); p27, copyright © Carol Ann Duffy 1990. Reproduced by permission of the author c/o Rogers, Coleridge & White Ltd, 20 Powis Mews, London, W11 1JN; pp31–32, © Khaled Hosseini, 2003, *The Kite Runner*, Bloomsbury Publishing Plc; p33, Michael Frayn, *Spies*, Faber and Faber Ltd; p45, 'Rain' taken from Michael Laskey's The Man Alone: New and Selected Poems (Smith|Doorstop, 2008); p47, copyright © Owen Sheers 2005. Reproduced by permission of the author c/o Rogers, Coleridge & White Ltd; pp51–52, copyright © Angela Carter 1979. Reproduced by permission of the author c/o Rogers, Coleridge & White Ltd; pp55–56, Tom Stoppard, *Spies*, Faber and Faber Ltd; pp60–61, 'Loveact' reproduced with permission of Curtis Brown Group Ltd, London, on behalf of Grace Nichols. Copyright © Grace Nichols 1983; pp61–62, Alice Walker, *The Color Purple*, published by Phoenix (an imprint of The Orion Publishing Group Ltd); pp63–65, (World, excluding Canada) permission kindly granted by Donald C. Farber, Trustee of the Trust u/w of Kurt Vonnegut Jr.; (Canada) "Slaughterhouse 5" by Kurt Vonnegut, © 1969 by Kurt Vonnegut. Used by permission of Random House, Inc. Any third party use of this material, outside of this publication, is prohibited. Interested parties must apply directly to Random House, Inc. for permission; pp65–67, (World, excluding Canada) Samuel Beckett, *Endgame*, Faber and Faber Ltd; (Canada) permission kindly granted by Grove Atlantic; pp69–70, © Sudha Bhuchar, 2006, *A Child of the Divide*, Bloomsbury Publishing Plc; p71, Imtiaz Dharker, *The terrorist at my table* (Bloodaxe Books, 2006); pp74–76, 'The School Among the Ruins', from THE SCHOOL AMONG THE RUINS by Adrienne Rich. Copyright © 2004 by Adrienne Rich. Used by permission of W. W. Norton & Company, Inc.; p92, (World, excluding North America) 'Funeral Blues' reproduced with permission of Curtis Brown Group Ltd, London, on behalf of W.H. Auden. Copyright © W.H. Auden 1938; pp93–94, (UK & Commonwealth) Arundhati Roy, *The God of Small Things*, reprinted by permission of HarperCollins Publishers Ltd © 1997, Arundhati Roy; (Canada) permission kindly granted by David Godwin Associates; pp94–95, Excerpt/extract from ANGELS IN AMERICA copyright 1992, 1993 Tony Kushner reprinted with permission from the publisher Nick Hern Books Ltd: www.nickhernbooks.co.uk.